CRK
Curt   15.MAY1997
3.5.90   -6. JUL 1995 Co. Hall   14. JUL 1998
SPEN . S.moore 21. DEC. 1995   14.SEP.2000
-1. AUG 1991 (13/8/95) -2. JAN. 1996
          16. AUG. 1995   15. JUL. 1996
17. NOV. 1992
19. DEC. 1992. -5. SEP. 1995   19 AUG. 1996
          25. SEP. 1995   -9. NOV. 1996
26. JUL. 1993 16. OCT. 1995 16. JAN. 1997
                              Wood
-6. APR. 1994   -6. NOV. 1995
                27 11.FEB.1997
24. JAN. 1995   17. MAR. 1997

The Disruptive Child

A Handbook of Care and Control

Molly Clarke

Northcote House

For Donald

British Library Cataloguing in Publication Data
Clarke, Molly
  The disruptive child: a handbook of care and control.
  1. Behaviourally disordered children. Care
  I. Title
  362.2'088054

  ISBN 0-7463-0576-1

First published in 1990 by Northcote House Publishers Ltd,
Harper & Row House, Estover Road, Plymouth PL6 7PZ,
United Kingdom. Tel: Plymouth (0752) 705251.
Fax: (0752) 777603. Telex: 45635.

Typeset by Kestrel Data, Exeter.
Printed in Great Britain by BPCC Wheatons Ltd, Exeter

Contents

Preface

This is a book for worried parents of a disruptive or difficult child
— not so much for parents who want to know *what* is wrong, or
why it has happened, but for those, often nearing the end of their
tether, who ask, '*How can I cope?*' It is based on many years of
personal, practical, proven experience and so the principles laid
down could also help teachers, educational psychologists, social
workers and other carers involved with disruptive children.

Some books about worrying behaviour in children concentrate
on different remedies for different kinds of problems. This book
is not like that. It is concerned with the practical management of
a disruptive child and my aim has been to look for ways of getting
on better with the child, to help him to change and improve his
behaviour whilst recognising that first you have to win his attention
and cooperation.

The book is based on the theory that behaviour is learned, and
the belief that parents can, and should, do something about
behaviour problems themselves. Behaviour problems can be helped
by the way *we* do things. There are suggestions for ways of
assessing what is going wrong, and how to plan changing things
for the better. In some circumstances direct intervention, but not
smacking, is discussed. It is always wise to begin gently, asking of
the child only what is necessary. Many 'disruptive' children do not
need very strong persuasion to change the way they behave. A few
will need a much more severe approach for a short time, but most
come somewhere in between. There are also suggestions about
dealing with some extreme problems which, while they may be

rare, may have to be faced. The importance of doing enjoyable things together is also stressed.

While I do not hold them responsible for what I have said, much of my own thinking was stimulated during the 1970s by reports from the Hester Adrian Research Centre at Manchester University. This Centre has done much pioneering work in teaching parents to assess, and devise training programmes for, their handicapped children or children with learning difficulties.

Two people have helped me by their painstaking reading of the book. I am grateful to Anne Pollitt for her thoughtful comments, and to Anthea Bruges for saving me from falling into some nasty pits. Both of them gave me time and encouragement, which I appreciate very much. My thanks also to Veronica Sherborne for reading and suggesting corrections to Chapter 4.

One final point. I have referred throughout the book to the disruptive child as 'he'. This has simply been for convenience and to avoid the use of such ugly devices as 'he or she', 'he/she', 's/he' and so on. I certainly would not wish to imply that all disruptive or difficult children are boys, and I am sure you will have no difficulty, as a result, in keeping your own particular child in mind as you read.

Molly Clarke

Introduction

MAKING A STAND

I'll start with the story of 'How I saw the Light' as it illustrates a point I shall be coming to. Don't be put off by its being about when I was a pretty feeble class teacher — I found the cure, eventually, and we shall be attending to the cure not to my experiences in school.

I used to line up my class in a corridor, waiting for the dinner bell. They were about fifteen years old and most of them were bigger than I was. I thought they were horrible louts. The corridor gave maximum publicity to the kicking and shoving that went on in the so-called line. As I told ringleaders to move to the back or the front, they protested loudly that they had done nothing and complained that I was always picking on them. On their unwilling way to whichever end of the line I sent them, they usually managed to knock someone 'accidentally' and start a scuffle. I prayed for the bell to ring and release me. Back after dinner I would let them know I was not pleased. No matter how I tried I could hear myself sounding like an imitation of Joyce Grenfell. The only difference between the trouble I had in the corridor and that in the classroom was that, once inside, at least I could keep the door shut. I hoped the rest of the world was not listening to my ineffective struggle against disorder and the surly reluctance to do anything I wanted.

One day the thought struck me that my class was having daily practice in doing the things I did not want them to do. They were rude, noisy and untidy and had no interest in their work, no matter how hard I tried to make it interesting. Their writing was disgraceful and other staff commented on the way they misbehaved as they moved about the school. My appeals to their better nature left them quite untouched and when I lectured them I might as well have saved my breath. Whatever I had to say always came after the crime anyway, which was too late. They were quite likely to find my criticisms funny, so in a negative way I was almost rewarding them for annoying me. Their behaviour and language were getting worse and I was perpetually worried. I exhausted myself with work and they watched me, doing nothing but make my life a misery.

The day after I experienced these revelations, I confronted the class in the corridor at dinner time. I waited until then because I wanted to choose my own time for the moment of truth and not let it erupt out of something one of them did. I also had to place myself in a position where, once I had started, I could not run and hide nor back down out of cowardice. It had to be public. I was nervous but I knew it was now or never. I told them to line up. At the first sign of approaching scuffles I told them, in a loud, if shaky, voice which could be heard all over the building, to get back to the classroom. They just didn't believe their ears. I said it again, louder, looking as much like a sergeant-major as I could, leaning forward as if ready for trouble. After a long pause they began to

shuffle disbelievingly back to the room. At the first murmur I shouted at them to be quiet. They were. I was astonished. I told them to sit down. They sat down. I told them to be quiet. They were. I stood them up again, in silence, and told them to line up outside in the corridor. As soon as they moved they started to talk, so back they came. By this time I was so far committed that my voice had stopped shaking. I had even kept the dinner ladies waiting — something unheard of in living memory. What was more, shouting by staff was strongly disapproved of in that school, but I had by now reached the point where if the head had given me any trouble I would have let him have it too. I might have stopped short of lining him up (I put that in in case he ever reads this).

Once I had got over the shock of what I had done I was further amazed by how still it was in the classroom when my charges came back after dinner. I found I was feeling strangely cheerful, but kept it to myself. I continued to imitate the sergeant-major. My little dears had better watch it; I had discovered the secret. I did not allow them to move, speak or think (almost) unless I gave them permission. 'Put your pens down when you have done question one and look at me.' They waited until everyone had finished question one. 'Pick up your pens and do question two.' If anyone even looked as if he was thinking of talking I was ready to jump on him. 'Put up your hand if you want to ask something.' They, who had been used to working in groups and helping each other, going at their own pace, talking, choosing what to do, moving round the room, were rocked. When I went home that evening, instead of feeling knocked out I kept on laughing. All I had done was **square up to them** and they had folded. By the end of the week I had realised that only about half of them were in truth bigger than I was. They had seemed gigantic. The surprising thing to me on that first day of the New Rule was that not only was I a lot happier, but so were my pupils. They were watchful but by the end of the day they had done more work than usual and we parted on the best of terms — *my* terms.

No dithering
From then on I kept a wary eye on what I was expecting the class to do and the way I presented tasks to them. I practised what I was going to say in front of the mirror, imagining how it would come across to them. I worked out everything they would have to do in the way of writing and maths etc, so that there would be no

time in which I dithered while they amused themselves sticking pins in each other. Nailing down my own preparation in much greater detail was easier than it looked. I set them smaller items of work which were meant to be got right without too much trouble, all leading in the direction I had been aiming for before but more carefully graded. The children were far more successful in their work. For a change they were pleased with themselves for getting things right; a rare experience. I had not read the books on behaviour modification then, but I set goals for myself and for the class which were within reach.

After a while I no longer needed to practise in front of the mirror but I did not forget about it in case of backsliding. How I looked and spoke obviously made as strong an impression as what I was saying. I learned with experience that everything about my attitude told them how I felt about something, and that what I said was only a part of what they were picking up. They had sensed that I had been afraid of them even though I had not admitted it to myself. I knew now that they were slightly afraid of me because they were unsure about what I would do next. I made mental notes about how to restore the present equilibrium if things should go wrong again, while being determined that I would not allow the old habits to return. I still went over each situation in my mind, to be sure that I made a strong enough impression on the class for them to obey me.

First, I had to get their attention and stop them messing about. I had to follow this quickly with specific things to do. I had to get them down to work without wasting time so I needed prepared materials to hand or the advantage I had gained would be lost. The message was that I had to **sharpen up my own performance.** Before, all my attention had been on their refusal to pay attention to what I said. I had to admit to myself that some of their previous bad behaviour had been of my own making, because I had been reluctant to give straight, plain orders which I expected to be obeyed. I had not even admitted to knowing the word 'obey' for years — it had been all reason and explanation and attempts to interest, persuade and motivate them.

ADULTS MUST TAKE THEIR RESPONSIBILITY

After that experience I never excused myself if I allowed children to behave badly. While they were doing that they were not learning what they should be learning but *practising what would harm them*. As a responsible adult it was my place to see that everything they learned from me would stand them in good stead in later life — in their attitudes to other people, their manners and honesty, their application to work, and moral values, as well as the skills I could teach them. What had come to me was the realisation that I had not been delivering the goods during the time that I had failed to control my class. By allowing them to behave rudely I had handed over to them responsibility for what they did while they were in school. Books on child development said, 'The child is right', and I had believed them.

Once the new regime was established it was possible for me to introduce far more interesting work than I had ever been able to tackle before because there were no longer any arguments in the room. The class knew I intended to manage them, and the time previously wasted in griping was put to constructive use. Their work improved from that day, partly because I now saw to it that they got it right. I changed the way I presented work to them, setting out in far more detail and in small steps what they had to do. Each step was a little more difficult than the last and they had to get down to it. One result was that they did not have to waste time doing corrections because I organised their work so that they got it right. We became fond of each other as we learned to respect each other. After things had settled down we had a lot of fun, which no-one could have pretended we did before. They stopped being horrible and there wasn't a lout in sight. I was surprised to find that they liked me far more now that I was capable of being, as I thought, horrible to them. There was no sign of resentment after the first shock; the reverse even. I began to think they liked knowing where they stood with me — and I am sure now that they did.

I had learned a valuable lesson which applies far beyond the classroom. No matter how many punishments you use, and no matter how severe they may be, when you punish someone you are always *following* something which has already been carried out successfully in spite of your opposition to it. Every time that happens the person doing it gets better at defying you, and at doing the thing you don't want him to do. At the same time your sanctions become less powerful. He finds out repeatedly that you can't really hurt him. If you stop him *before* he does something wrong, that same person gets his practice first in obeying you and secondly in doing things the right way. You can then follow his action with praise instead of with recrimination. He can see for himself that what he did came out right, so he can enjoy his own success and does not depend on you alone for satisfaction in his achievement. For the first time he begins to associate you with pleasure and finds that you are not so bad after all; you actually help him. Once you reach that point you are in a different game because each of you can show respect for the other. He becomes a different person because he sees himself as someone who is capable and responsible — and so do you. You can both hold your heads up.

The significant and frightening thing is that unless the adult who should take charge does so children and adolescents do not make the right decisions for themselves. How can we expect them to? They do not have the experience of life which tells you what to expect based on what you know. They do not imagine the possible outcome before doing something and stop themselves when necessary, unless they have been taught to think in this way.

My experience in class illustrates that without **direction from a responsible adult** children will do what the strongest personality among them tells them to do. As long as you shirk from playing your own part, that strongest personality will not be yours. In a nutshell, if you do not give the orders someone else will do it for you. If you leave your own child to decide limits for himself, he has only his small experience to guide him. That will not stop him giving you your orders, because he does not know the extent of his ignorance. If you allow this, you dig a pit for yourself.

Writing from my own experience

During the much-maligned sixties young people's attitudes changed, from expecting the answer 'No' from adults unless one had permission, to expecting 'Yes' unless given a reason. Whether the sixties were the cause of all our present trouble or not is not significant now because while we spend time looking back we are not doing anything about the present. What matters very urgently is what we are doing now about children and young people who are still in our care at home or in school and how we fulfil our duty to them. That is all we have any influence over, no matter what went before, who was at fault or what the child inherited in the way of characteristics. We have to start with what we have got, here and now, and do the best we can. What we try may not turn out exactly as we would have liked it but once we have made a start we can improve as we go along, adapting what we do where necessary as we watch the progress we make. We have to take action about children who do not respond to ordinary friendly discipline at home or in school — who are, in a measure, **disruptive.**

My observations were made during many years of working with disturbed children and adolescents, a number of whom were mentally handicapped. The work was carried out in schools, a college of education and a residential unit. Where mental handicap was present, it was not the cause of the unacceptable behaviour although it certainly made the behaviour more difficult to handle because language was not as well developed. Unacceptable behaviour is not confined to one group, one social class or one ability level.

What follows is an accumulation from personal experience, reading what the experts say and listening to them. It is the result of many years of watching and working with others, with varying degrees of success, always trying to find the answer which suits the individual. The prime concern of this book is with urgent problems of behaviour management, so it starts with **first aid** in that area and goes on later to **general issues** in child management which may help to provide strategies for avoiding serious problems.

I hope that by making practical suggestions I shall be able to encourage some parents, teachers or carers to look at child management from a different angle, one which gives the initiative to the adult and lets him or her see that it is not compulsory to carry on forever in a relentless and seemingly hopeless struggle — a struggle in which the adult appears no stronger than the child. The disruptive child shows by his behaviour that he cannot organise his own responses. He needs someone to do it for him for the time being, to keep him secure while he learns better ways. And this applies equally whether the child is causing minor or severe disruption.

Health warning

Most of what I have to say throughout the book applies to any disruptive child. Where specific reference is made to the management of **extreme** behaviour problems (as in Chapter 3), the suggestions should *not* be adopted before being carefully examined and, where necessary, modified. It is always best to start with the mildest and smallest doses of the mixture, to give it a chance. Only when weaker medicines have been tried and have failed should we turn to the stronger stuff — and that is not for use with young children in any case.

I
Disruptive Behaviour

WHAT IS DISRUPTIVE BEHAVIOUR?

The *Concise Oxford Dictionary* defines 'disrupt' as 'shatter, separate forcibly', and 'disruptive' as 'bursting asunder'. It defines 'behaviour' as 'deportment, manners, moral conduct, treatment shown to or towards others'. In other words, something that a person does which can be seen, heard and felt, and which affects other people. So disruptive behaviour is behaviour which affects others badly and, consequently, affects badly the one who is behaving in a disruptive manner.

Disruptive behaviour can be so to a lesser or greater degree. There are few parents or teachers who spend all their waking or working hours in a life-and-death struggle with a totally disruptive child. There are many who have to deal with unacceptable and aggressive behaviour from time to time. The principles outlined in this book can be adapted by anyone who is involved with children who are difficult to control.

The same principles apply to children and young people with far more severe problems, who display what is called '**challenging**' behaviour, that is to say, behaviour which is extremely difficult to manage, disturbing the child himself and everyone around him, and very resistant to change. The term covers the more extreme forms of disruption which may occur in severe mental handicap, or in severe learning difficulties, or in special care. Such children are sometimes to be found in special schools and may be causing problems even there. The problems often persist into adolescence and sometimes beyond. However, in writing about '**disruptive**' behaviour I am referring to noisy and persistent temper tantrums; screaming; spitting; scratching; pinching; kicking; punching; biting; headbutting — actions which may actually injure others — refusing to comply with reasonable requests, for instance, to sit quietly at mealtimes; tipping furniture over and even damaging it in temper; throwing plates of food on the floor. Disruptive behaviour does not cover self-injurious behaviour nor problems arising as a result of severe or multiple handicap.

It is likely that any child behaving in a disruptive way will be functioning below his own ability level and may not be using language very well. But it is the behaviour and the child that are important to us, not whether there is also a handicap. The difference between a healthy child and a handicapped child as far as behaviour is concerned is not one of kind but one of *degree*. Underneath they are much the same, but some are far more energetic about their unacceptable behaviour and hang on to it until a far greater age than others.

I have also learned that **freedom of choice** cannot be used equally well by all children. Some may have to be shown how to make a choice and others to accept that for the time being the choice will be made for them. At least that way they can experience getting things right and receiving praise. It is not morally wrong to step in firmly and stop a child who is doing something wrong or behaving in an unacceptable way, but it is asking too much to expect him to know what is wrong without showing him. And he may not have the capacity to stop certain kinds of behaviour by himself. The disruptive child cannot organise his responses.

DO THE UNDERLYING CAUSES MATTER?

Not much space here is given to searching for the underlying causes of disruptive behaviour. Most of our energy should be devoted to seeing where we are now and trying to improve things in whatever small ways we can. It is not suggested that underlying reasons for difficult behaviour are unimportant or insignificant — far from it. But we cannot alter anything that has already taken place and, while it is of interest because of what it has done to the people concerned, all we have to deal with now is the person as he is today. If what he does is harmful to himself or to others we have a duty, if we are responsible for him, to influence his way of behaving and persuade him to change his habits.

For our purposes 'behaviour' is something we can see and therefore something we can compare with how it was last week or last year. We can count how many times it happens and time how long it lasts. We can look at what actually happened before and after and think whether by changing something we might be able to improve the outcome. We may even find that something we are doing ourselves is having the opposite effect to the one we want — we know what to change in that case.

Time spent in searching for *reasons* for this behaviour which arose in his past will not necessarily **improve his self control.** It is also dangerous territory for the untrained and we are far safer when we confine ourselves to what we can see and count. Studies of disturbed behaviour which involve remembering past events and evaluating them depend on a fairly well developed understanding and sophisticated use of language. The majority of children and young adolescents whose behaviour causes concern are not sufficiently articulate, although they may pick up some of the jargon. These factors make one wary of treatments based on individual interviews, discussion and insight, and experience shows that such approaches often take a very long time.

ARE ADULTS TO BLAME?

No child behaves disruptively — to any degree — regularly without putting in a period of practice. The question is, *what* were other people doing while he practised? *Why* did they not stop him long ago and see that he learned something more acceptable? A question more easily asked than answered, and carrying the suggestion that, because they did not stop the child, the adults are to be blamed. Blaming people is always a pointless exercise and doesn't change the problem.

People who have problems in managing their children usually do everything they can to sort them out and when they do not succeed they take it very much to heart, seeing themselves as failures, set apart from others. In doing so they undermine their own efforts when what they need is an injection of confidence and some positive help. So instead of apportioning blame time would be better spent in encouraging adults to consider their influence on the children in their care.

Having a hand in the upbringing of children, whether one's own or other people's, requires thought and attention. It is not enough just to be oneself. The adult, whether parent, teacher or relative, must rearrange his or her life and patterns of behaviour to **protect the interests of the child.** We cannot escape from influencing the way the child develops by our example, by the way we speak, what we encourage and what discourage, and by what we communicate to him via our radar or whatever it is that tells him how we feel before we even know it ourselves. Adults should be aware of the kind of experiences they offer, and what children are likely to derive from them, and be responsible enough to control situations, for instance unsuitable subjects for discussion until children are out of hearing.

Make sure you know, too, what the child is doing when he is away from your influence and intervene when you do not like the sound of it. Children do copy their friends, or the biggest noise in the group, and sometimes they are not physically strong enough to defend themselves against doing so. If we leave them to get on with it we abnegate our responsibility and take a chance on what they pick up. They can't always discriminate. They need to compare new ideas with those which they know, from standards set at home, are right or wrong so that they can judge whether to accept or reject. When they are developing children adopt the rules of the family and live by them later on so where there are no rules the child has nothing to live by. The Jesuits were not far wrong when they said the first seven years were the formative ones. In the end it does come back to the parents, the authors of their children's existence and their protectors in a threatening world. Others will be able to help, but the only way to be sure something is done properly is to get on and do it yourself.

OTHER RELEVANT FACTORS

Love

A fashionable belief is that provided one has a 'loving relationship' with a child only good and positive things will flow from that. The implication is that we do not have to take any special action in order to promote that relationship. Any reasonable person would want this, but unfortunately it does not occur of its own accord nor without our putting a great deal of thought and hard work into it. When you love someone you **act responsibly towards them,** even if it means preventing them doing something they want to do. It also means often giving up doing something you want to do yourself and always being aware that your own behaviour is making an impression on the other person and watching what you communicate to him by word or by conduct. It is not enough just to love a child and keep him happy. We have to see that he grows up in the right way, otherwise we will find that it takes more and more to keep him happy, and he is never really satisfied even then.

The trouble with a disruptive child is that he takes the love and all that comes with it, but he draws the line at fulfilling *his* part. He does not recognise, perhaps because he has not been taught, that something has to come from *him* as well. He does not value the love, nor the giver. He does not say, 'Thank you', he says, 'Is that all you can do for me? Only that?' We have to intervene because that is no way for him to go through life. To think of himself as the receiver only, is to live without a concept of himself as someone who can contribute to the world around him and take an active part. He needs to change the way he sees himself.

Firmness
Before we can do any good with this child however, we have to put a stop to the unacceptable way he has been carrying on. This will involve us in being firm, even quite unpleasant, with him, for if you can't stop him when he is small and doing something which will hurt him, he is in trouble. The hurt may be running into physical danger, or practising the habit of ignoring you, but whatever it is somehow you have to find a way to interrupt him and make him attend to you. Once that is understood, and you can stop him when *you* want to, you can provide him with things to do which are acceptable and especially things he will find really enjoyable — things for which you will be able, truthfully, to say 'Well done!'

It will not take a long time to change direction, but you will have to be strong and vigilant and keep it up once you start. After all you are not an ogre, just a wise adult who has lived a lot longer than he has. You are prepared to take trouble, time and thought for the sake of his future happiness. To make excuses for him and let him carry on doing things you know are wrong is to endanger his future, not yours. He is not just a naughty child, he is not 'bad', he was not born unable to be good. What he has done is to *learn* bad habits and *practise* them to perfection. He has to be helped to change the way he behaves because what he does at present is not acceptable. But let no-one pretend that this is easy, least of all for his mother, for she has been accustomed to behaving in certain ways herself in relation to him. She, and probably the rest of the family, will also have to change. All this will take **persistence and attention**, every day.

Repression and free expression

There was another fashionable belief, similar to the one about loving relationships, that children must be allowed to *express* themselves and on no account be repressed or all sorts of damage would be done to the child and he would grow up inhibited and unable to make or sustain relationships. All around us now we see the results of free expression. Too much freedom is a mental threat to young children, who cannot control their own emotions or behaviour without sympathetic support. It is only with time and the experience of being controlled that they develop an internal code, which tells them when trouble lies ahead, and which sets off warning signals, stopping them in time. Given complete freedom they do not think first what the consequences are likely to be if they follow a certain course of action.

To use a simple example, provided with as much paper and paint as he wants a child, unsupervised, will end up covering himself and everything round him in paint, possibly throwing it around the room. He will enjoy the action so much and get so excited that he will not look for an end product nor bother about the chaos. No ordinary home or classroom can tolerate this wild use of painting materials, and the next and likely step is for the child to be excluded from painting/clay/any other kind of art work. This is not the way to teach him what to do, but it is the way of the world. What he needs is adults who will impose order on the proceedings from outside, so that he can get on with the job safe from pandemonium. He needs a set-up in which he can practise handling the materials while someone else takes charge of his behaviour. Under close supervision he will be allowed to feel quiet inside himself, in a way which only comes from control. Only then can he attend to what he is doing with paint. Finger painting and splodge painting by all means — *but* sitting down, all surfaces protected, one colour at a time and finish after one or two goes. No chance of big spills, no scrubbing all the colours together into a dirty grey, no yelling and throwing paint around and definitely no footprinting. Other than **controlling the situation**, no-one wants to dictate to him what he actually paints. Once he has had a chance to see what it feels like to use the paints without creating mayhem he will want to do it quietly for himself but, unless someone shows him, how is he to know what he can do with paint?

EDUCATING FOR CHANGE

So, having understood a little more about the nature of disruptive behaviour and the factors which bear upon it and influence it, we are better placed to consider how to change that behaviour, how to teach a child new and better habits.

If you have a disruptive or difficult child in your care decide to do something *positive* to improve the way you manage him. To encourage yourself, face the facts — even at his present age he is causing you a lot of trouble over ordinary everyday things and you spend too much time in hassle. If you don't do something about his behaviour no-one else will. Or if they do you won't like what they do.

I learned through the experience I described in the **Introduction** to face up to signs of trouble even when afraid, and to do something positive to stop it and change the outcome. This approach applies to behaviour problems at all levels. Not to hope the problem will go away by itself — because it won't. Not to have a discussion and democratic vote — because 'they' will act undemocratically. Not to pretend there is nothing wrong — everybody knows there is. Not to expect someone clever to deal with it — people you consult often turn out to be less clever than you are yourself. Face up to the situation you are in and determine to tackle it.

To help you arrive at the best course of action the next two chapters outline the principles for assessing the problem, and for working out strategies for improving and overcoming it.

Bear in mind, too, the **principles of education**, applicable at any level from the simplest to the most advanced, which will form the basis for teaching new habits of behaviour:

● Start the learner on familiar ground where you know he will get it right.

● Introduce new ideas one at a time, showing how much they are like things he knows already.

● Tackle only one small new thing at a time.

● Make sure he gets it right by the way you show him.

● Show pleasure at his success and praise him.

ASSESSING THE PROBLEM

You will not have reached the present point with your child without having tried gentle methods of persuasion. Most children respond to loving care with the occasional reprimand. Those who do not do so are likely to have experienced a time when their parents have ignored bad behaviour and encouraged good, hoping by doing so to establish an acceptable level of management in the home without constant disagreement. When this fails, parents are not sure what to try next, feeling that the next stage is likely to be more oppressive on the child and not relishing the thought. They know they have to do something positive, because if they let things drift they may find themselves unexpectedly losing control and lashing out at the child in temper. But losing control or taking wrong decisions which make things more difficult for the child are more likely to come about if parents don't take stock of the problem first. Making an **objective assessment** of the situation when you are living through a very traumatic period can seem like a waste of precious time and energy, but the effort will have been worthwhile when you arrive at a clearer plan for remodelling your problem child.

When you have encountered a tantrum or some other form of 'punch up' consider what happened. Stop and think what started it and what you did yourself in response. Could you have got, say, a half or a quarter of what you wanted without a row? Would it be worth asking for less just to put yourself in the position where you can be pleased? At least you would end up with some advantage, however small.

If we allow ourselves to be rushed into a confrontation out of irritation or escalating disagreement, we are likely to find we have a brawl on our hands from which all participants emerge with resentment. This develops into a kind of self-perpetuating chain with one event triggering another and no satisfactory outcome. If the chain is to be broken *you* will need to take the initiative. If you think out your strategy first you can attend to the business, not get caught up in a fight. Thinking about causes and effects and jotting down what you see is happening (not what you *think* is happening), will make it possible to bring about improvements which should lead to the Great Revolution. You will be able to look back and see what usually starts things and which of your treatments works best.

MAKING YOUR ASSESSMENT

Now for a really useful tool. It will change the way you think about your child and *your* problem, that is *his* behaviour. It involves keeping a record of what is going on, on charts which you make up to suit yourself.

Life can be divided into BC — Before Charts, and AC — After Charts. Say you are having worries about tantrums. **Before Charts**, if someone asked you how you were getting on and how the tantrums were, you might have said, 'They go on all day. We do nothing but struggle and fight and I usually give in from exhaustion in the end. I'm at the end of my tether.'

After Charts, your answer to the same question might easily be, 'I've been keeping a record. They seem to happen just before lunch and at bedtime. There are other times, but these are regular. I'm going to try giving him his midday meal earlier and letting him get to bed earlier and see whether that makes a difference.' Now you have found what looks like a pattern in the times of the tantrums and you could even count how many, in order to make weekly comparisons and monitor his behaviour.

But the chief benefit is that you are no longer at the end of your tether. The simple effect of starting a chart is that you have moved from being one of the fighters in the ring, to becoming the referee (who does, admittedly, get punched now and then). You have been making notes as an outsider would have done, without being drawn into the struggle. You will inevitably get on better as soon as you place yourself outside the drama, because you can now decide what you are going to do about it. It may not work, but at least you have given yourself the advantage and you can always try something else if you need to. It is in *your* hands, and that's the difference. You are the one who gives the orders and so you should be because you hold the responsibility.

Charting the child's behaviour

A chart is simply a piece of paper stuck to the wall. Note the date and the details of what it is you are charting, in our example tantrums, as shown on the next page.

Tantrums		Date:_____
Time	Small tantrum	Big tantrum
8.oo am		
9.oo am		
10.oo am		
11.oo am		
12 noon		
1.oo pm		
2.oo pm		
3.oo pm		
4.oo pm		
5.oo pm		
6.oo pm		

Put a tick or a cross for each tantrum against the time it happened. If there is **a pattern** and you find they occur at about the same time every day, near a mealtime for instance, you can ask yourself whether your child is hungry, and try changing his routine. If that doesn't help, is he wanting, and perhaps deserving, a bit more attention at certain times? If you decide to give more attention, be sure to do it *before* the time the ructions usually start or you will undermine what you are trying to do. If you were right in your assessment of the reason, and alter something as a result, things should be easier at that time of day. But allow time for the new routine to become established and don't become discouraged too soon.

Planning a coping strategy will be easier if you can establish not only when certain situations occur but more about what may be *causing* them. You may think you know why but a little scientific observation can be quite revealing. Instead of thinking you know what starts the trouble you may be able to say that for three out of four episodes a particular thing happened just before the start and perhaps it was that which did it. Now you are in the position of deciding whether to change it, or let the child know he just has to put up with it. The difference is *you* are the one who is manning the controls, not the child. But remember, it is not always the child who is the offender. For instance, did we interrupt him when he was engaged in doing something and without warning insist that he stop and do what we wanted? In our example of tantrums adapt the chart so that you can note not just the time but also the events related to the tantrum, just before and just after it took place:

Tantrums	Date: _____	
Time	What happened just before?	What happened just after?
8.oo am		
9.oo am		
10.oo am		
11.oo am		
12 noon		
1.oo pm		
2.oo pm		
3.oo pm		
4.oo pm		
5.oo pm		
6.oo pm		

By means of such a chart you can also examine the pattern of events just after the ructions. If you triggered the tantrum by saying 'No' to the child, and then you ended it by giving way, you should think about **changing your tactics**! What you may learn is that something you did after the tantrum, without realising it, was enough to encourage him to do it again. Children — and adults — don't usually keep on like this unless it pays off in some way. All we have to do is rumble them. It is not always easy to find a reason, but searching for it is a more profitable enterprise than letting a small body tread all over us.

The **length of time** a tantrum lasts is important, too, and it helps the way you deal with it when you are aware of the passing minutes. Whatever happens you don't want to let them run on and on. Then no-one knows what the dispute was about at the outset, only that now it is a contest to see who can last longest. You reduce yourself to a place of equal power with the child, which is no way to change his behaviour. So spend a little time with the pencil and paper and the watch. Become the observer for a while and add another column to the chart to record the length of each tantrum.

Charting your own reactions

By charting the *child's* behaviour you have begun to see if there is a pattern associated with the tantrums and any connection with the 'befores' and 'afters'. But before you can plan your strategy for

Tantrums		Date: _____
Time	Tantrum	What I did
8.oo am		
9.oo am	X	Went on washing up
10.oo am		
11.oo am		
12 noon	X	Shouted at him (busy)
1.oo pm		
2.oo pm	X	Picked him up and cuddled him (had more time)
3.oo pm		
4.oo pm		
5.oo pm		
6.oo pm		

dealing with the child's behaviour you need to look at your own reactions — what did *you* do while he was having a tantrum?

Did you do anything to make it worth his while to throw tantrums? You ignored him once. You showed him you were cross once. You showed him you approved of the tantrum once by picking him up and cuddling him. Whether you were busy or not only affected you; it made no difference to him. He won't be keeping a score of what you did along these lines, and there is nothing to tell him whether you dislike his behaviour or not, judging from your reactions. He may see no connection at all between what he does and **how you respond.**

If you want to cure some of his more annoying ways, start by examining your own reactions to him when he offends and how you respond when he pleases you. As soon as you make sure he gets the same kind of reaction every time he displeases, and a very different one when he pleases you, you should be on the road to improvement. If we want others to oblige us we have to have discipline ourselves. Perhaps if, after assessing your own reactions, you decided to ignore him each time he started he might wonder what had gone wrong with you. And if you kept it up he might decide, given time, that that particular sort of carry-on did not pay and try some other way of gaining your attention — especially if you fell over with delight every time he was good.

Your strongest line is to find ways of giving attention whenever he is being good and to get that in before he turns to crime. One thing many of us do is take well-behaved children for granted. We say nothing, or if asked say, 'Well, of course you're good, I expect you to be good.' How grudging we are with praise. A little judicious appreciation goes a long way, even for very small signs of willingness to do what we want. Every one of us blossoms under encouragement. Why should a child be different? The point to remember when we are wanting big changes in behaviour is that changes come in very small instalments. If we are not satisfied unless we get the whole lot right away, we are on to a loser and might as well give up. Accept a move in the right direction and you can persuade and ease him along without losing sight of your aim. Without declaring war. Just taking a little longer. It makes life far more agreeable for everyone. Try to spend more time in noting the good things and plan to leave less space for the rest.

The value of charts
Completing charts can be a chore, but it is worth persisting for a

while because the result is a different way of thinking and a much more **objective approach**. By becoming more detached you place yourself in a position where you are the one in charge, which is where you ought to be. By putting a few things down on paper you get them out of your head and you have something more than your feelings, which vary with the state of the struggle and your own tiredness, to guide you. How many times such things as tantrums happen, how long they last, what seems to trigger them off or encourage them, are facts you don't know without assessing, and won't remember without pencil and paper. And, once you can put your hand on the information, daily or weekly comparisons become possible so that you can **monitor the child's behaviour** as a whole.

ANATOMY OF A TANTRUM

One thing is true for all of us — the more we practise doing something, the better we become at doing it, whether it is picking locks or playing the violin. If an adult allows himself to be drawn into a daily struggle with a child over something that just has to be done, like cleaning teeth, he will be giving the child practice at resisting his authority as well as resisting the cleaning of teeth. To give way, or bribe the child, is to play into his hands, teaching him how to manipulate the adult in ways he would not have thought of for himself. However the situation arises, the adult who is involved needs to look at what he is doing and make some changes. In this, the adult and child are performing steps in a well practised dance:

Parent. 'Now let's clean our teeth. Open wide.'
Child clenches his teeth and makes noises of protest.
Parent. 'Come on now, be a good boy. Open your mouth.'
Child starts yelling.
Parent, taking a tighter hold. 'Don't you want nice clean teeth?'
Child, trying to get away and yelling. 'No!'
Parent. 'If you don't let me clean your teeth you'll get toothache/ they'll all fall out/you won't get any ice cream/we won't be able to go to the zoo and that won't be very nice, will it? Don't you want to go to the zoo? As soon as we've cleaned your teeth we're going to the zoo.' Etc.

By this time the child is screaming and producing tears. The parent

then tries to comfort him by offering this or that toy accompanied by the following dialogue:

'Would you like this one?' 'NO!' 'That one?' 'NO!'

And so on, accompanied by the child kicking, throwing objects, flinging himself down on the floor.

Change the subject and the venue and such a scene can be quite a draw at the supermarket. All the time the parent is asking for cooperation, but inviting the child to say 'No!', which he does with practised accomplishment. A common thread running through behaviour problems is that the child cannot stand having to do what someone else wants him to do, nor having to wait for what he wants, nor having to accept the answer 'No'. It goes without saying that something needs to be done before the child gets too strong to manage.

As a result of developing the habit of assessing situations, rather than being driven by them, we can analyse the typical tantrum in some detail. It begins to look as if there is more than one participant in this game, as if the parent sometimes feeds the lines to the child, almost expecting the answer 'No!'. Not all the child's complaints and opposition, whether spoken or not, are unreasonable — while he gets the blame because he plays up, the adults around him are often the cause of the trouble without recognising what they are doing. This is why assessing the problem can be so helpful — it highlights aspects the importance of which the parent may not have been fully aware of and which can be improved immediately by a

change of approach. Already the first steps in your strategy for change are evident.

Developing a strategy for change

A child is more able to change his behavioural habits if he feels secure and certain of the basic ground rules. The child needs you to set the rules up and keep him to them. He can't do it by himself, but when you do it he feels safe because of the rules. One way to cut out some of the ructions is to make sure he *knows* what is going on and what is expected of him, even if his understanding of language is limited or apparently non-existent.

- Develop **a daily routine** which he will soon recognise and accept. Do things in the same order when you are dressing him, or getting ready to go out, going to bed or preparing for meals. Have a song to go with the activity and turn it into a game, 'This is the way we comb our hair.'

- Use the **same simple phrases** to go with everyday activities every time you do them.

- Make **some simple rules** for both of you to do with essential things, and stick to them no matter what. Not too many, but enough to know that if it was 'No' yesterday, it will be 'No' today and tomorrow. (No turning on the hot tap. No touching the cooker.) Some of us grew up with 'No dinner, no pudding', or 'No play before homework'.

- **Be enthusiastic** when he does something right. Let him see you are overjoyed; hug him and kiss him and make a fuss (don't give him a sweet).

- **Don't be disheartened** if he seems not to be able to learn something. He may do better if you give it a rest and go back to it after a while. Sometimes children seem to make no progress at all at something and then suddenly find that they can do it after all. Perhaps their internal computer took it in but had to sort it out first.

- Remember that until they have had quite a lot of **practice at a new skill,** children may not see the sense in doing it at all. But rather than giving up, they still have to go through the process of learning the skill because it is after learning that the understanding comes.

- **Try not to interrupt** the child when he is concentrating on something. If you really have to, at least give him a few minutes' warning. If you make a practice of giving, say, five minutes you will give him a chance to finish properly, which is an encouragement to start in the first place. He can also put his things away the way he wants to, in peace. In doing this you show that you do respect him and his efforts.

- **Allow him time to finish with an activity mentally** as well as by clearing up. Don't demand attention instantly to the next thing if he is apparently still focused upon what he has just been doing. Talk to him about it and encourage him to remember what he was doing. This is a welcome sign that he is thinking and remembering, which is how we learn new things ourselves.

Many outbursts of anger are caused by adults who do not consider the child's activities sufficiently important to be respected, who interrupt without thinking and who expect immediate attention to themselves. And yet we complain that our children do not concentrate!

In developing a strategy for change it is worth thinking about **how long** you ought to allow a confrontation to continue. We don't always win every battle the first time and sometimes lose more than it is worth by going on too long in our insistence on perfect obedience. Perhaps we would achieve more if we asked a little less and so provoked less opposition. That way we would more quickly get to the stage of being pleased with the child, the point at which he begins to see that it is worth changing his behaviour habits. But there is a difference between deciding to ask him to do something we are fairly sure he will do anyway (rather than demanding something he won't want to do) and letting him get away with something in spite of what we want.

If you find the child keeps up a tantrum for as long as ten minutes you must seek a way of stopping it because that is too long, but you want a way which does not force you to give in after you have made a stand. You may find that walking him up and down outside until he calms down and the tension is reduced will work for you. The thing is that you do not wish to punish him, nor to quarrel, but to have him comply with a reasonable request.

However, it does happen sometimes that you just have to climb down or risk being inhumane. You might acknowledge privately that you will put up a fight for a time only and set yourself a time limit in advance of trouble, for instance three minutes, beyond which you will not persist. But let it be known that your attitude to whatever caused the trouble in the first place remains unchanged and that you will oppose it every time it surfaces.

2
Tackling the Problem

DECIDING TO ACT

Making the decision to tackle the problem is always the worst part. It requires the courage to come out in the open about what you truly think, even if by doing so you invite opposition. *Doing* what you have decided is simple by comparison. The moment you take the initiative with the child you yourself decide on the terms of engagement. You think out the implications first and satisfy yourself that there is no danger of losing your temper, or acting against the interests of the child by hurting him or using excessive punishment or excessive isolation. You ensure you keep within what you know to be acceptable by making notes (on daily charts) of what you are doing. You **plan a deliberate course of action** — which is certainly preferable to haphazard punishments, constant nagging, reproaches and general dissatisfaction with the child. None of these is controlled and in none of them do you keep an eye on your own performance and what effect it is having on the child and other members of the family.

You will realise then that you can't change your strategy in secret; the world will see and comment. Such openness is especially helpful for other children in the family, who should see you put a stop to what is not acceptable (but be careful that they do not get involved in scenes which they misunderstand). So, be prepared to brazen it out. Decide that if you have trouble in public you will remove the offender from view if possible but you will not back off once you have started. Get out of the bus and make him walk home in the rain. Make your stand in the shops. Be sure, if there is a fracas, no-one will offer to help. Don't hear them if they say, 'Oh, the poor child'. Comfort yourself with the thought that letting him get away with it never stopped him, but consistent intervention and action will in time. You will find life is more peaceful in between the ructions once you have made a stand. Plan to extend the harmonious spells to squeeze out the others.

United in action

Bear in mind that anything more firm or severe in your method of dealing with your child brings ethical issues with it and you have to settle these in your own mind and with your partner before embarking. It will not do to have another close adult letting it be known by word or conduct that you are going beyond their support.

They need to understand that there is no question of your being hard on the child, nor unreasonable, nor unkind to him. That if you adopt a tough attitude it does not mean you will hurt him, even if you use physical strength to prevent him doing something. It means, 'I will not let you go on damaging yourself like this any more. What you do matters to me.' It would be a great advantage to the child if you could rely on support. Passive resistance from the other adult(s), which broadcasts itself silently through the ether, counts as active opposition and will undermine what you do. It does not help the child because it intensifies the lack of consistency in his surroundings. What is he to make of it? He cannot depend on anything. Even the adults go different ways.

Remember that the child is not the only one who has the problem. Everyone in contact with him suffers in some way as a result of it and some of them contribute to it. You might think that all that is needed is for the child to change, but the assessment and analysis you have made will probably show the part of others, both in the causes and also in sharing the consequences. Someone in the household may be afraid of him or of his noise, even if they have not expressed it in words, and may give in to him when they know they would not do the same for his brother or sister. If he picks this up on his radar, what does it do to him? Does he trade on it? Or does it terrify him into further outbursts in panic, attempting to force someone to take control of him? So we can see the importance of a **consistent, united approach.**

Ignoring the critics

Having discussed with adults in the family what you intend and the reasons for the decision, and being firm in your own mind, you can privately counter any outside criticism, which you are sure to receive, by asking yourself how well the critic would do in your place. You could also ask whether they have the child's interests at heart or their own feelings about what the neighbours think. This is especially trying if your child has a mental or physical handicap; the instinct is for everyone to feel sympathy for the child and let him get away with murder while he is small, and to turn their backs on him when he is older. There is even more justification for doing whatever you can, within acceptable limits, to reduce anti-social behaviour in this case.

It doesn't matter what other people think or say about what you do when you change the way you have been handling your child. You will be careful not to do anything remotely unkind even while you have of necessity to act very strictly. The fact that other people don't like it probably arises from their not having the responsibility that you carry, and perhaps not having faced problems in the way you have had to. They go home and forget about it, leaving you questioning whether you are right. Don't let it affect what you have, with careful thought, decided to do. Your job is doing the best you can for one particular child, not pleasing friends and relatives. If what you do is **in the interests of the child**, and you know you are not being unjust or inhumane, you should go ahead.

DEVELOPING YOUR PLAN OF ACTION

From your assessments so far you will probably have found that
several problems appear to contribute to your child's disruptive
behaviour, but it would not be sensible to tackle more than one at
a time. In addition, you may be tempted to decide on the most
worrying aspect of his behaviour and to go all out to correct that.
However, the better way would be to sort out all the trouble spots
and select the one which causes the *least* friction. In dealing with
it you will meet less resistance and therefore be more likely to
succeed, and you can then go on to the next trouble spot. Usually,
once you have sorted out the easy problems the others seem to be
less overwhelming and may even melt away by themselves. It is
when you try to face everything at once that it all seems equally
important and pressing, and above all impossible. When things
look like that make a list — worst at the top, least worrying at the
bottom — and *start at the bottom.*

At the beginning of this book I spoke about how I had struggled
with an unruly class without success. The way I broke into that
and forced them to attend to me was by shouting at them and then,
once I had the children's attention, telling them what to do and
making them do it — I saw to it that they obeyed me. I did not
ease up for several weeks, and then only gradually. I never left it
to the children afterwards to do as they liked without direction.
Without being shown, how could they know what to do, or how
to do it?

If your child's behaviour is such that you have to do something
equally drastic yourself, the '**shout and give orders**' method,
plus lots of love and encouragement (and keeping him to what he
is told to do), provides the basic strategy.

First, you have to stop him in his tracks and make him attend
to you. Then, it is no use talking about what you want and what
he should do and what he did wrong — you have to take some
visible action which leaves him in no doubt that you are changing
all that and that you are now the Chief and he is the Indian. Do
something drastic which can be seen. Stand as tall as you can, raise
your voice, pull an ugly face, shout at him to stop, and make him
actively do something different. If you are in company, make sure
that everyone around hears you and if necessary hears him too —
and especially *sees him do it* ('Sit down!', 'Stand up!', 'Wait!',
'Stop!', 'Look at me!' or some other short instruction).

As soon as he has obeyed your first command, give him

something else to do ('Pick up all the papers you have dropped') and insist that he does it straightaway, properly. The minute he gives signs of complying with what you want and stops yelling and thrashing about, your whole attitude changes and you resume normal service as if nothing had happened. You have no quarrel with him, only with the ructions. But you don't talk about it. It has gone. There are no recriminations. Out comes the sun and on you go. You are not interested in punishment or nagging, only in getting on with the day. What went before has gone and is forgotten as if it had never happened. You get on with enjoying the rest of your day, but ready to pounce like a tiger if he shows the slightest sign of behaving badly again.

Don't stop in the middle of all the bother to tell him that you do love him really. What you have shown him up to now cannot properly be called love. You have neglected his interests though it may have been wrapped up as allowing him free choice of activity, or sharing responsibility, or something like that. The way to love him is to get him on the right track however unpopular it makes you, and not to let up when he grumbles. In a very short time this will give you an experience you have not had before, that of a settled relationship where each of you knows what to expect from the other and is able to get on with the job in peace. You can see the child's **self-esteem** rising as a direct result of higher achievement through discipline. Everybody uses less energy to produce more, and has a happier time doing it.

Putting your plan into action

First of all make sure you **choose the right time** to put your plan into action, not when you are tired or feeling at your wits' end. Children have an uncanny knack of picking up what mood we are in without a word being spoken. If we choose a day when we are feeling particularly low to tackle a member of the family about some habit we cannot stand because finally it has become too much for us, we hand it to him. He can see us coming. We show him what it is that gets under our skin, what to do now to provoke us. So, in order to get what you want, don't allow yourself to be rushed into a confrontation against your better judgement.

The theory is to choose *one* thing he does wrong, but not something he will fight to the death for even if that means ignoring a more serious problem for the time being until the habit of obedience has been established. The object is to tell him what to do right instead of what he was doing wrong, showing him how to comply and making sure he gets it right. Assuming he is being noisy about your request — in this example, getting dressed to go out — or has openly defied you, you would go into action like this:

1. Get attention. **Shout** 'Stop!'
2. **Look** as if you mean it.
3. **Tell** him to do something specific. 'Sit down.' (Wait) 'Pick up that shoe.' (Wait) 'Give it to me.' (Wait) 'Hold out your foot.' (Put his shoe on)

   If he does not obey any one of these instructions, after a reasonable wait on your part, repeat it, louder. If he yells back, repeat 'Stop!'. Make a big cutting-off movement with your hand.

He has now stopped whatever he was doing and attended to you and done what you told him.

4. **Be ready** with something different for him to do, something immediate and easy. 'Put your coat on.' (Hold it out to help him) 'We're going for a walk. That's better. Come on, let's go.'
5. **Remain firm and determined** to the end of the scene — not, 'Would you like to go for a walk?', not, 'Do this puzzle while I get on with the washing up.'

He needs your full attention throughout to make sure he gets the message, which is that you give the orders and he does as he is told.

Once out and walking, provided he is quiet, be perfectly normal. Just have it in mind to march him straight back home if he tries anything on, and if that happens act against it immediately. Do not give him warning and do not threaten. If you do have to be firm, even harsh, keep it short and simple like the example. Don't give him something to do as the alternative (stage 4) which you know invites refusal.

Remember that for every unacceptable thing you stop you must offer him a way of being in favour as soon as he complies. If he gets the idea that no matter what he does he is always wrong, he will see little point in cooperating and may choose defiance instead.

You will be able to be pleased with him more often if you ask for things he can do, and do right, even if they are not particularly demanding. For instance, if your instruction to him to pick up his shoe from wherever he threw it down is likely to cause a further battle, it would be better to keep simply to 'Stop!', 'Sit down.', 'Hold out your foot.' The point is to contrive that he pleases you and you don't want to try and pretend that you are pleased when you are not satisfied. Ask less so that you can reward more (and use encouraging words, a kiss or a cuddle as a reward, rather than sweets).

When putting your plan into action, don't

● **lose your temper** — recognise it if you are becoming wound up and stop;

● **hurt** the child;

● **use excessive punishment** (see comments on pp.42-4 about punishment);

● **operate in a haphazard manner** — keeping notes and charts will help to prevent this.

Keeping it up

It is the responsibility of the adults to keep things fairly steady most of the time, and to bring them back under control if they start to get out of hand. A child cannot be expected to recognise danger signals and on his own take decisive action to restore control. He becomes consumed by the force of his emotions, and once uproar begins his actions intensify the strength of those emotions. This is not the case for his mother, father or teacher. They are not vulnerable in the same way. They see it coming. Usually before a tantrum starts there have been smaller failures to comply with your reasonable requests, and you have the chance of stopping the rot before it goes any further. A child may not recognise the signs and may just be overwhelmed by the sudden rush of anger.

For this reason it is not usually possible simply to *ignore* disruptive behaviour, by sending the child to his room to cool off for instance. How do you ignore having your shins kicked? Or get him to his room, probably upstairs, while he is having a go at you? If you manage to shut him in his room, or send him to bed early, what does he do while you wait for him to recover his equilibrium? If he wrecks the room, what next? We have to accept that there are times and children for whom the gentler methods — ignoring the occasional outburst — simply do not work.

With such children, if you decide to stop a small infringement you must be prepared to keep on stopping it for as long as the child chooses to keep trying. Even all day. You won't have to do it all day every day, but it is the **consistent approach** which will save you from being driven to treating him unkindly in an outburst of anger. Most of the time you will probably only have to speak firmly to achieve what you want, but it is the knowledge that you are prepared to do more that will have the effect on him. Above all, any restraint or punishment should last the shortest possible time, only long enough to establish who is boss before resuming business. The activities you have ready for him when he calms down need to be far more interesting than looking for trouble with you, more attractive and therefore worth his while.

According to the scale of misbehaviour we won't always have to use our full plan of action, happily; there are other ways of making your wishes felt and some of them are worth practising in front of the mirror. See how you look when you stand as if you are angry, and have your 'dreadful look' handy if you feel the need to be ready for confrontation. You can usually stop threatened trouble by looking angry, but you want to be sure you appear capable of being ready for anything. One look at you may be enough to make him change his mind.

If the dreadful look is not enough, a shout is preferable to a wrestling match. Or making the child stay in a designated spot for a time, standing in the corner facing the wall, for instance, or sitting him down on the floor ('And don't you dare move!). We may not like taking such action but the object is to interrupt the cycle of disruptive behaviour. Whatever method is used, the whole thing comes down to the **strength of mind of the adult,** and his or her ability to communicate by their actions that they mean what they say. They will have their way no matter what the child tries. Their manner also tells him that by behaving as he is doing just now he is in absolute disgrace.

PUNISHMENT

Should punishment form part of your plan of action? In working with disruptive children I have found little use for punishment, reproach or blame. Such things come too late, they are not related in the child's mind to the crime, they do not repair the damage and they may only arise out of the adult's own desire to let off steam. It is better to get on with the job. Punishment given now for what is past will not stop something which happens without premeditation tomorrow. Our children are not professional crooks. It is up to us to keep our eyes open tomorrow. Extracting a penance from someone who has offended keeps the memory of the offence in mind and I would prefer to get him to do things the right way and then go on to whatever comes next. If he is to dwell on something let it be what he does that is right, not wrong.

A very sound argument against punishment is that it is hard to find a form which does not make use of some activity you would rather he enjoyed, or one which you don't get dragged into yourself. That is why a **fixed penalty**, as described below, is best — 'You did such and such and you know it is wrong. Now you have got to do X to make up for it.' (Not, 'You know it upsets Mummy to hear you speak like that'.)

There is, though, the occasional exception in a child who does go in for deliberate provocation, which he has learned somehow brings its own negative reward. It may be necessary to use punishment with him, but only if he has at least a basic grasp of language, sufficient to understand what you say to him about this.

Another time when it would be right to punish a child is when the other children in the family need to see that justice is being done, for example, when a child does something out of spite, or dishonesty. Other children will know very well if we let someone off when we should not do so.

A fixed penalty would be preferable to arbitrary punishments if the child offends frequently, for instance if he throws his dinner on the floor he gets no more to eat until the next meal, only water to drink, and he cleans up the mess. You may have to hold his hands to make him do it, but do it he must. No need to talk about it either; it is the action that counts. If he creates in someone else's house you whip him out and home and he misses whatever is the next thing on the programme — drink and biscuits, TV, story. It's hard on you because you have to miss the visit too, to see that he does. Another way is to give him something to do to make up for his crime, like tidy something up, wash pots, be in when he wants to be out, or out when he wants to be in. If he knocks furniture about then he should be made by you, probably holding both his hands, to replace every single thing in the room in its correct place, including things he did not upset, until you are satisfied that he has made good three times over. No chatting. It should be a very long and tedious chore and you should insist that the room is perfect in every detail before you let him stop. This is a worthwhile form of punishment as there is something good to see at the end of it even if it took half the afternoon.

It is not a good thing to use food as an item for argument,

persuasion or punishment. The only time it would be appropriate to withhold food is if he throws his meal on the floor in temper, and then food should be withheld only until the next normal mealtime. But on the whole it is dangerous to make an issue out of food — you can't withhold it for long but the child can withhold eating and get you over a barrel.

TAKING STOCK

What happens when you think you have done everything right, and it doesn't work? If you have given time for new routines to become established and you don't see much improvement, don't get disheartened. Perhaps you need a fresh perspective — try working through this checklist:

● Make sure you have diagnosed the problem **correctly**. Compare today's observations with those you made when you first started.

● Look for areas where there has been improvement, however small, and those where there has not. If you can see any improvement, **concentrate** on that. What are you doing that is successful there? You need more of that recipe and not so much of the others.

● Compare your goals or aims today with those when you started. Ask yourself whether you are being **realistic** in what you hope to achieve. The fact that you are having difficulties suggests that you are asking too much at once, or it is too hard for the child to do. Or that you are not explaining clearly what you want.

● Try asking for less, and be careful not to insist on perfection. Remember to **manipulate** things so that it is easy for the child to do them right, and that he gets some fun out of what he is doing.

● Use a **light touch**; don't be too earnest. Are you shouting too much? Remember the purpose of a shout is to interrupt something and to redirect attention to what you want done. After that you should go back to being quiet. Otherwise you will both just get louder and louder, competing for the place of top dog. Not what you intended at all.

● Check the notes you made before and update them. Maybe

your circumstances are different now and you need to **revise** what you want to do. He may be bored. You may be. You might decide it is time for a change of emphasis, to make life more entertaining. Don't give up but perhaps leave what you were attempting for a little while and go back to it again later.

● You might need to adopt some more concentrated methods of working, especially if the child is getting bored and needs something more **demanding**.

● Are you doing as much as you should to balance your 'training' demands with activities designed to develop the **affectionate** element in your relationship and to build trust and cooperation (see Chapter 4)?

REDUCING STRESS IN THE FAMILY

There will be times when you will feel pretty worn down by the whole struggle yourself and what it does to everyone else in the family as well. You are bound to be quick on the draw now and then, when you don't mean to be nasty really — expecting other children to jump to it; biting off the head of the Beloved; a tendency to scream at the lot of them as you fling down the casserole. Accept that such things *will* happen in a family under stress and that as part of tackling the problem you will need to work towards a **stable and stress-free** home environment. Be aware of the danger points in advance so that they don't take you by surprise; indeed most of them can probably be avoided by encouraging an open atmosphere in which the problems the rest of you encounter can be discussed between you.

If you are a single parent coping alone, try to keep an objective eye on your own danger points and take heart from the knowledge that anyone else in the same situation would be likely to experience stress, too, so ease back on that sense of failure. You may think the rest of the comments in this section won't apply to you, but the underlying principle will — don't allow yourself to be isolated by self-condemnation. There are details of helpful people to turn to in Chapter 6.

The children
It is a good idea to speak about your feelings to the other children

when the air is quieter. Being honest about the problem, explaining how you are trying to deal with it and how difficult you find it, at least shows them you know they have a lot to put up with and that you appreciate the help they give. Give *them* a chance to say how it affects them too — you can understand them feeling permanently fed up at not being able to do the same as their friends and never having any peace at home. Don't be surprised if some of the following **resentments or fears** surface:

● A sense of unfairness, when one gets away with murder and the others don't.

● A feeling that you're being dishonest — pretending it's not all that bad really, or he can't help how he behaves, when they know it's bad and they think he can help it.

● Not being able to bring friends home.

● Or keep their own things away from him.

● Or do homework in peace.

● Or sleep in a room by themselves, away from him.

● Not being able to explain him to their friends.

● Being afraid he will hurt them.

● Or that the adults won't protect them from him.

● Or that the adults themselves are afraid of him.

● Just being afraid of him.

● Feeling embarrassed about him.

● Being teased at school.

● Having to support the adults when it makes them angry to do so.

● Being jealous of all the time he gets from parents.

● Actually being physically hurt by him.

● Worrying that there is really something seriously wrong with him that is catching.

● Or that they could have inherited it and will pass it on to their own children when they grow up.

● Or that it is too serious to be spoken about.

● Having to take part with the adults in managing him when they are still children themselves.

● Perhaps having to babysit and not having sufficient authority over him.

By giving them a chance to say what they feel some quite deep-seated resentment and fear can be talked about in a loving and supportive atmosphere and can be cleared away.

You may need to take a look at how *you* are managing your disruptive child, especially if other children are young or timid. If we are the kind who dislikes arguments, who tries always to be even-handed, neutral, tolerant, open-minded, always allowing the other side fair time, we may find to our dismay that we are actually allowing our problem child to take advantage of the other, more polite, children. What he does may even amount to bullying or browbeating them. We have a responsibility to them too. Try to deal with noisy ructions away from younger or timid children, so that they do not feel threatened themselves, or somehow that they are to blame, or that they will be next in the receiving line. But make sure that they see that we do not ignore wrongdoing, and don't let them down when they need your protection.

Your partner and you
You are probably familiar with some of the following problems:

● Exhaustion.

● Disagreements.

● Mutual reproaches/criticism.

● Tension.

● Guilt over something done/not done, not admitted/cannot face being admitted.

● Searching for someone/something to blame.

● Fear of inherited defect.

● Unsolicited advice from relatives, neighbours, friends.

● Fear of losing your temper with the child and hurting him.

● Feeling trapped, that there is no peace from the fight whichever way you turn.

Your partner is probably going through the same feelings. You can bolster each other by not keeping the problem to yourselves all the time. Talking about it will probably make you **less critical** of each other, because to know that each of you appreciates the struggle the other is going through takes some of the sting out of it. You are both in it together, so don't blame the other. It's not a question of fault, there is a problem to be solved.

Talk about the least difficult of your worries and see if there may be a better way of dealing with them. Some of the rest will grow smaller once you make a start. Don't throw away your energy in bad feelings — use it sensibly.

Remember that children model themselves on their parents. Show them that responsible parents **support** and look after each other, especially in caring for their children.

But remember, too, not to waste time and energy in condemning yourself if stress does erupt. Plenty of people scream at their perfectly ordinary children all the time, in between slugs of gin, and take no interest in their welfare; and the children seem to manage without suffering great damage to their psyches. Children have survived being sent up chimneys and down mines. Even if you have done things you now regret, given the same circumstances, other people would probably have reacted in the same way. So put it behind you and start again, don't take it out on yourself. Your child is pretty resilient, as you can see by how strongly he resists your efforts to reform him. It is enough if you just **keep going**, pegging away. You don't have to be the Wonder Parent who never made a mistake. You'd be very lonely — there aren't many about.

Finally, the harder the struggle the more we need to **get away** from it at regular intervals. There is great refreshment in taking up some kind of study or hobby which is quite different from anything you have done up to now, and which leads you into attending classes, starting on something new, learning a new skill, perhaps getting a qualification, having to think about ideas altogether different from anything connected with life up to now. It is not selfish to think of doing something like this — it could be a lifeline.

3
Dealing with More
Difficult Problems

Almost everything I have to say about children whose behaviour
is disruptive will have application to children whose behaviour is
unusually difficult. The principle is always for the adult to stop
what is unacceptable and show what is wanted, with lots of praise
for the slightest move in the right direction.

But in tackling the more difficult or extreme ('challenging')
behavioural problems the suggestions should *not* be adopted
without careful examination and whatever modification may be
necessary to suit the particular child. They would not be suitable
for very young children. By **difficult** we mean behaviour which
is causing a lot of worry but which is still containable, whereas
extreme or challenging behaviour would mean that the child
(who is probably older) would not be manageable in an ordinary
school and may even be causing problems in a special school.

A CHILD UNDER PRESSURE OR UNREASONABLE BEHAVIOUR?

If you decide you will have to go further than shouting and giving
orders, the method discussed in the last chapter, make sure you
have assessed the situation correctly before proceeding — look for
other signs because there may be another cause.

There is a difference between a single, uncharacteristic outburst
of aggression (the next step in escalating behaviour problems), and
noisy and possibly violent displays which occur whenever a child
is frustrated. The single outburst suggests that the child **cannot**

cope with something, that he is being overloaded or over-stimulated, or is too tired to do what he wants, or what you are asking of him. He may not be well. He may be afraid. At school he may know he ought not to eat something because he is allergic to it, but not be able to communicate this to the adult in charge. Any number of things could be behind it and we need to look at signs other than the fuss he is making before plunging in and assuming that it is wilful misbehaviour. If, for instance, he is generally more jumpy and irritable than he used to be, he could be under pressure somewhere which is not doing him any good. We don't want to take it out on him in that case.

The aggression which is an expression of anger at frustration, a refusal to cooperate, an inability to wait, is in a different category. It merits serious attention while the child is still small enough to be handled by one adult, because it disrupts family life and will not go away by itself. A few — a very few — children may display aggression as a result of a medical condition. We are concerned here with children, some of whom may be receiving medication, but who are not otherwise a health problem. This is not to suggest that ill-health permits outbursts of uncontrolled temper, but it may make them harder to deal with.

It would be wrong to suggest that there is one recipe for all conditions and children, that the strategy for dealing with mildly disruptive children would apply in equal measure to those displaying the more difficult behavioural problems. The children in the latter category seem to be tougher than their parents, disrupting their lives and dominating the home with their demands. They keep going until everyone else is exhausted from the effort of coping with their unreasonable and unpredictable behaviour. Onlookers are amazed that their families seem to continue to love them; that they make excuses for them, putting up with the mayhem. Sometimes the parents are unreasonable in demanding that other people see their children as they see them, expecting others to make the same allowances. When they do this it seems they have lost sight of reality and are being drawn into self deception. These children have learned a way of life which members of their family, unintentionally, keep going. It is not healthy for any of them; if the parents are wise they will take a look at what they are doing and see what they can do to change habits which are causing so much harm. After all, these children have shown that they are capable of learning; it is *what* they have learned that is the trouble.

When you wipe a tape you leave a blank. Try it with a human being and you don't know what will appear in its place, but it won't be a blank. We want to exchange bad for good. To give all the encouragement we possibly can to any sign the child gives of doing things we approve of. We do not want to be unpleasant all the time, but to lead him with as little fuss as possible to behave in a different and more agreeable way. It is up to us to make it attractive to him and to show our pleasure when he moves in the desired direction. But because we are now thinking of more difficult problems we know we may have to act more decisively until we bring about an improvement.

DIFFICULT BEHAVIOUR: SEVERE TANTRUMS

Let's start at the deep end with putting a stop to tantrums that may involve **outbursts of aggression** so that we can steer the child into better ways of treating us and himself. We know tantrums thrive on attention, and that unfortunately it is difficult to ignore them, especially if they include hurting someone. You cannot ignore a child who is kicking you and screaming at you, perhaps trying to do more. Or who throws the dinner you have just given him on the floor in rage and punches you when you try and make him clean it up. In defending yourself you give him time and attention. By being prepared for the outburst, you may manage to make it *less satisfying* for him next time he tries it.

You must stop him hurting you, or others, or damaging furniture. This probably means you have to hold on to him to restrain him. If that happens, you should try to avoid looking at him while you do hold him, or at least avoid looking at his eyes. Do not allow yourself to become disturbed by what is going on; do not join in and make a fight of it, though it can be a temptation (as one mother said, who had allowed her anger to dominate, 'If I'd touched him I'd have killed him!'). Let him see, when he looks at you, that you are the one in charge, not him. You show this by the way you hold yourself, the tone of your voice if you speak, and the look on your face. Make sure you show clearly by the expression on your face that you don't think much of him. If he is shouting and yelling there is not much point in joining in, except perhaps one shout when you grab him to shock him into stopping.

Don't get into an argument with him and if he tries to start one just don't answer. Do not be sweet and reasonable and try to talk him out of it. Say loudly, not caring who hears you, 'Stop!', 'Stop it!' and hang on until he does stop, properly. A large cutting-off movement with your hand will emphasise what you are saying. If you have a free hand, that is. Wait until he stops thrashing about — until he does so, hang on. You don't want to hear what he wants, and you are not going to let go, nor argue about it. You don't change. You are waiting for *him* to change, and eventually he will. You should not let him go if he is still determined to attack you, even if the tantrum lasts longer than the three minutes suggested earlier. Don't dish out the encouragement until he is quiet and ready for the next step — it will come. But while he is playing up you should look as unpleasant as you can manage.

The minute he shows signs of stopping, release him and carry on where you left off before the blow-up. Don't ask for or expect an apology. Behave as if nothing had happened. The minute he makes a wrong move again, back you go immediately. No warnings. No explanations. Just stop him. He cannot afford to have you give way to him. It is only *your* firmness and strength that save him from chaos and he can't get out of it by himself, however easily he got into it. Be fierce with Granny, he is not her poor lamb. You can listen to her later. She'll have something to say when he is older — along the lines of, 'Where did we go wrong?' — if you don't take steps to curb him now.

It is important not to try to reason with him or talk him out of his tantrum. Not, 'What's happened to Mummy's lovely boy then? Come on my love.' Not, 'What's upset you? Tell Mummy what's wrong.' Not, 'You'll miss your trip to the zoo. Don't you want to go to the zoo? I thought you wanted to see all the animals.' None of that. If you start on the zoo tack or on any other kind of enticement, what you are telling him unintentionally is that it is up to him to decide whether he goes to the zoo or not; that when he condescends to stop the racket you will be waiting to take him where he wants to go. Will you? Is it right that you should when he has been carrying on like that? It is not up to him — you are the one with the authority to make the decision and you won't be taking him anywhere at this rate, not unless he shuts up pretty quickly, and makes it convincing too.

If you do take him wherever you were supposed to be going, you want to feel satisfied that he is going to behave when you get there, because if he starts over again once you have passed the turnstile you will have to abandon your entrance money and come straight home. You would really like to take him and have him

behave in a way in which he could enjoy the visit, but you should perhaps settle for a less ambitious project just now. In fact, a quiet walk around the block looking at gardens and whatever there is to see would be kinder on both of you than any outing which can be used in bargaining and public demonstrations of an embarrassing kind. Sometimes by attempting less you can manage to enjoy each other's company instead of having open war.

Your matter-of-fact manner when facing a noisy outburst, and refusal to bargain or even talk until he has stopped, is a help to him. One part of him wants to get you as upset as he is, to spread all round him the disturbance he feels inside. But the other part of him is afraid that you are not strong enough to stand up to his rage and keep chaos at bay. You should be honest with him in showing your contempt for these shows of aggression, but also let him see that he cannot make you lose control of your own feelings no matter how hard he tries; and no more will you lose control of him. He has not the power to upset you in this way.

Staying firm and in control yourself is the essence of managing him and bringing his behaviour under reasonable control. Everything else you can do to reinforce him in all the positive aspects of his day, to enable him to get on happily with others and manage his feelings himself, will contribute to improving the quality of his life. None of that can begin to flourish as long as he is allowed to upset the boat by throwing a tantrum every time someone says 'No'. You might say to yourself that he can have a tantrum if he wishes, but he does not disturb the household while he does so, only himself. He might even have to watch others go out while he stays behind to cool off. If so, do not make a song and dance out of it. Just let him know quietly when he has settled that it is too late now for you and him to go. You don't need to say any more. They will come back and talk about where they have been and he will hear all about it. Far more effective than nagging and it doesn't create an unpleasant atmosphere all the time.

EXTREME OR CHALLENGING BEHAVIOUR: AGGRESSION

Restraint is going to be more important within this context so we need to consider carefully what we mean by it and where we draw the line between what is acceptable and what is not. It is generally allowed that one should use only as much force as is necessary to bring the other person under control, and no more. Any way in which you hold him must therefore be enough to keep him reasonably still without doing any damage to him and he must be released as soon as he stops trying to injure you.

When managing a child who is attacking you physically you could find you had to do more than just hold on to his hands while he raises hell. If he tries to hurt you by biting or kicking, it would be better to hold him from behind. He is likely to do less damage and he misses the satisfaction of seeing your face. This may sound pretty drastic, but there are children and adolescents who do present very difficult problems and who do really hurt. The thought of bullying or physically hurting a child, weaker than you, is abhorrent and we are not considering anything like that. But occasionally **physical intervention** is the only option, and if we have to use it we must remember that we are stronger and heavier than the child. In other words, be aware of what you are doing and ensure that if you decide to restrain him in certain circumstances you do no more than is essential to prevent injury. The danger to watch out for is any feeling of anger within yourself.

Restraint itself is not a punishment but literally a holding operation. If the need to restrain is likely to occur frequently read a book on self defence, written by a professional, and pay attention to techniques which you can use to prevent your opponent hurting you without hurting him. The law states that no more force should be used on him than the degree of force which he is using against you. You have to think how you will use that, which is another reason for keeping cool and planning ahead. It should be stressed again that such strategies should not be used with young children. A reminder here, too, about the use of charts. Once you think in terms of direct physical intervention it is important for your own peace of mind to keep a record of what you do so that you can check you have everything under control.

There are some children whose understanding is so restricted that occasionally their outbursts of anger seem to be outside their own control. What can you do when you are faced with that situation? People like nurses, whose jobs sometimes bring them into situations like this, are advised how to hold without risking damage to the other person. This is to prevent things getting so out of hand that someone will be really hurt if the situation is not brought quickly under control. You should not tackle a problem of this severity without medical advice on all aspects of the child's health and behaviour, but if you do have to take drastic action here are some things to watch: When he goes for you your first instinct is likely to be to grab hold of his hands and feet, which he is using to hurt you. Instead, it is safer to wrap your arms tightly around

his upper trunk near the shoulders, pinning his arms to his body. If there are two of you one person can hold around his upper arms and the other around his thighs. That way you can stop him while knowing he is safe, but watch out for your own head and shins. You may have to hold him face down on a mat if he is hurting you but that brings in complications because he can then hurt himself by banging his head. The danger in holding his hands is that if he really struggles to get free he may break a bone. This underlines the need to be aware of the principles of defending yourself without hurting the other.

Once you have the child under physical control then the principles outlined for dealing with severe tantrums would apply to this situation also.

CHALLENGING BEHAVIOUR: PROBLEMS WITH TRANSPORT

A very common area of difficulty concerns transport, especially if someone other than the parent or carer is doing the transporting, for instance if a child is attending a special school. Although going to school is a great event in its own right, if you can't get the child there without other people having problems then the event becomes marred and traumatic. Problems over transport need to be anticipated and looked at long before school. It is for *you* to see that your child behaves properly. It is not reasonable to ask other people to pay special attention to the behaviour of one child and overlook the interests of the other children. They are engaged to maintain safe procedures over all, not to specialise in one.

Whatever the vehicle is, and however disturbed a child may be for whatever reason, it is imperative that he **sit quietly in transport.** If he has made a habit of playing up as soon as he gets into the family car, the chances are that he will be taken out in it as little as possible because of the driver's concern that there may be an accident. While this can be understood easily enough, it is unlikely to improve the child's performance. If his behaviour is unsatisfactory in the car, he needs practice in travelling the *right* way. The worse he is, the more practice he needs, but it has to be managed so that what he practises is what he ought to be doing.

If your real worry is about straightforward safety before you tackle anything else, because he throws himself about in the car and protests vigorously, you might consider a safety harness which is more substantial than an ordinary seatbelt, but which must have an instant release buckle. There are some to be had, but if you can't find one look at sailing harnesses. The release must be as quick as that on a standard seatbelt and as easy to reach. The harness itself should not confine him beyond preventing excessive and dangerous movement, so it should have room for him to move backwards and forwards in his seat but restrain him from standing up or lurching about, especially in the direction of the driver. You might arrange it so that you can put the harness on him before getting him into the car and then fasten it to its anchorage when he sits down. You want only one unlocking device and if that is round his body the anchorage can be fixed to the floor. Whatever you do about this, ensure that the harness does what you want but still conforms to standard safety practice, that everyone who uses the car understands how to operate the release, and also that it can be seen in case of an accident.

In giving the child lessons in travelling by car your purpose is to **establish safe behaviour,** not simply to go for a joyride. You do not need to take a long time over each lesson. There should be two of you, you to deal with the child and the other adult to drive. First sit the child where he can't reach the driver and keep to the same place each time he goes out while he's learning. If he starts thrashing about hold him so that he can't do any damage. For the first time just go round the block, stop and get out. That's enough for the first attempt. Repeat the lesson the next day, and every day if possible, gradually extending the time spent in the car. At the first sign of trouble during a lesson say, firmly, 'No! Stop it!' Look cross and sound cross. Use your hand to make a sharp cutting-off movement to show you mean it. Wrap your arms around him, holding his arms inside, if he tries to snatch and grab. Keep it up — it won't go on like this for long and soon you will be able to be pleased with him, even if there is only a little improvement. Once you win a little ground you can afford to ease up a bit, but be wary. Be ready to praise him when he cooperates, even a little bit, letting him know you are pleased and that he is wonderful, rather than telling him he ought to have done even better. But if he shows a desire for the old, bad ways, back you go again.

Whilst concentrating on teaching your child to travel properly, continue to deal with any tantrums that may arise as outlined in previous sections. However, if you are in danger of losing control of the child stop the car and take the child outside to deal with the tantrum (provided you can hold him securely enough for safety beside the road). If it is not possible for the driver to stop immediately then hang on to the child until he quietens, but it would be better not to contemplate a car journey of any distance whilst there is the possibility of a major blow-up. In an emergency a knowledge of the holds used in professional self defence would be a great advantage.

You might prefer to write down what you plan to do and keep a note of how you are getting on:

Aim: Good behaviour in the car.
1. Get child used to wearing harness while pottering about the house.
2. Decide which seat he is to use and arrange anchorage.
3. Tell him you are going out in the car.
4. Expect him to get in by himself and sit down. If he refuses, pick him up and put him in his seat.
5. Hook on.
6. Drive off on 5 minute journey. Behave as if he is expected to be quiet and talk to the other adult.
7. Get out without commenting on how he has been. Mention something you saw perhaps.

● Always keep to the **same routine**, in and out. If he has been good, give him a hug, but don't go overboard — just, 'Good boy!'

● If he misbehaves, **restrain** him if necessary but do not comment on it. Say, 'Stop it! No!'

● If he begins by misbehaving but then shows **improvement,** be lavish with the hugs and kisses to make sure he knows he is appreciated.

Some people give a child a favourite toy or small object to play with in the car, to occupy him. The danger with this is that the day is bound to come when it cannot be found and all hell is let loose. Like all of us the child has to put up with being bored sometimes while going from A to B. If the toy becomes all-important and you can't make the journey without it, you allow him a weapon for bargaining about his behaviour. It can be as bad to have travelling songs to stop young passengers from getting fed up. You may be in trouble if you can't think which tune it is your increasingly furious young passenger is demanding. We may entertain children or sing to them for a time but every child has to learn to be quiet in traffic or when the driver wants silence, and this applies to the disruptive child. After all, who will sing his favourite song to him if he ever has to go in an ambulance or to school by special transport? And finally, never bribe with sweets because that is to invite terrorism.

THE DIFFICULT CHILD: TOILET TRAINING

Toilet training is often a problem with the more difficult child, but don't be daunted because it seems such an elementary skill which he should have picked up as he grew out of babyhood. As with any other problem, plan your campaign of training and

Toilet training	Date:		
Time	Wet	Dry	Soiled
7.00 am			
8.00 am			
9.00 am			
10.00 am			
11.00 am			
12 noon			
1.00 pm			
2.00 pm			
3.00 pm			
4.00 pm			
5.00 pm			
6.00 pm			
7.00 pm			
At night			

coping, remembering to plan it so that you achieve being pleased with him. Use a chart, especially with a younger child, like the one on the previous page, to establish your **best training times.**

Checking your child on an hourly basis and completing the chart will soon show you when you need to catch him and will save spending all day in the loo. Sit him on the loo for a few minutes only at those times. Don't expect results at first, ask only for cooperation from him. Just be pleased that he has sat there and if he should, by accident, oblige, fall over with delight. Be lavish with praise and tell everybody how clever he is.

Don't make a great toil out of it all; it would be better to try this routine twice a day for six weeks than every half-hour for one day.

If toilet training persists in being a problem, check through these points:

● When he is wet, does he feel uncomfortable, or are his clothes so warm that he hardly notices? Some children like the feeling. It is only when they are cold that they complain. Might he find it more worthwhile to use the toilet if you left him to feel cold and wet and uncomfortable for a time?

● When he is soiled, do you give him a nice warm bath with bubbles in it? Instead of the warm bath, would a businesslike, only just lukewarm shower, with no chat and no eye contact, be less attractive and more effective?

● If he gets all the fuss when he does the right thing, and the minimum contact and reward when he does the wrong thing, he might decide to change his ways.

● With an older child there is no reason why he should not wash his clothes and his sheets, as long as it is dealt with in a matter-of-fact way. Appeals to his better nature, reproaches, asking what other people would say, or what he'll do when he's 20, are unlikely to have any effect. Having to wash a sheet is the real consequences of the action — end of story.

4
Aids to Improving Behaviour

What we have been concentrating on so far with our disruptive child can be termed **first aid,** interrupting or stopping the wrong behaviour and seeking to establish the right, teaching the child the habit of responding in obedience to our discipline. But our aim is to get to the point where our child is able to **motivate himself** towards better habits of behaviour, where he can be self-disciplined and controlled in his responses to his circumstances. In moving our concentration away from first aid in one area towards treating the whole child, there are many means at our disposal for improving his approach to life, whether through increasing his language, building up his cooperation, trust and confidence, or improving his self image. And we can do so much through play, through activities we can actually enjoy doing together.

LANGUAGE

We regulate our own behaviour by using a kind of internal commentary on what we are up to. This includes listening to the arguments for and against our actions, the rights and wrongs, in our heads. We think things out in words although we do not usually say them out loud. We prefer one course of action and reject another on the grounds of its being right or wrong. We may picture what has happened in the past, or imagine what other people would think about what we intend. We carry on or not, according to the direction in which our thoughts have taken us. Whatever images we see in our mind's eye, the weighing up and deciding are done using words which we imagine we hear, spoken by ourselves.

It does not look as if our child uses this machinery very well. More as if he sees pictures of what he wants, without hearing any voice telling him that one attraction is all right but another will lead to trouble. He does not show signs of being able to *choose* between one thing and another in his mind, but instead rushes for whatever is irresistible because, having seen it or thought of it, he wants it — and he wants it now. So improving the way he uses language will encourage the habit of thinking first, which will become a means of defending himself against rash impulses. The aim is to **improve language** through specific practice with emphasis on key words to control disruptive behaviour.

Learning to choose

Start by showing him how to **make a choice.** We ask him to do this all the time, but perhaps our words don't mean the same to him as they do to us. 'Do you want it or don't you?' usually means 'I can't wait all day'. 'Make up your mind!' usually means 'I can't wait all day'. 'Are you coming or aren't you?' usually means 'I can't wait all day'.

You can see from these somewhat exaggerated examples that we broadcast by our tone and look that we want to get on to the next job, which obscures the meanings of our questions. It makes everything look like 'Hurry up!', yet we expect the child to understand what we mean. If he does not recognise our words then he is left to guess what we mean by the expression on our faces, our tone of voice, or what we do. We may take something away from him when he is slow to choose, thereby removing choice; or pick him up and carry him because we can't wait. Such actions on our part do little to promote better understanding. It is worth spending time on showing him *how* to make up his mind, showing him what it is you do when you choose between one thing and another.

Instead of just giving him a drink, for instance, of milk at mid-morning, we can give him a choice and take pains to show him what happens when he chooses. For that to register with him, action has to follow his choice straightaway and we must emphasise what he has said. (Don't fuss too much about refined manners; one thing at a time.)

Hold out his cup of milk in one hand and one of orange juice in the other. Say, 'Do you want milk or orange?'. As you say 'milk', hold it towards him. As you say 'orange', hold that towards him.

When he tells you, or points at or looks at one, you give it to him and take the other one away. You say, 'Milk, please' as you give it to him, and remove the orange, and that is that. You say it, to show what is expected from him, but don't demand that he says it just now.

The other drink, which he did not want, you have yourself or put out of sight so there is nothing to begin an argument about. Nothing visible anyway. That's it; no persuading, no changing his mind — it's gone. He chose what he wanted and he's got it. With practice he will find he has power, through making a choice, that he did not have before. It is not the power to start a fight, but the power to get desired results by going about things in a certain way. He deserves praise.

If he does not want anything, or refuses to join the game, or tries to grab, he can go without (give him some water if he feels thirsty in a little while). Whether he has a drink or not is for him to decide, but you do as he says quite pleasantly. Then you put everything away until the next meal. Both of you go on to the next item on the agenda. Offer the same choice, in the same way, in the middle of the afternoon. It may take about a week to become established before you begin adding further instalments and there is no point in trying more until the first routine is settled. 'Good' and 'Clever' help.

The next choice will be something small to eat, not for nourishment but to show that his wishes do count with you in that department as well. But the object is to *show*, not to discuss or explain. You could offer a biscuit or small sandwich; nothing to interfere with his meals. As soon as he shows which he would like he gets it without waiting or fuss. 'Do you want biscuit or sandwich?' 'Biscuit, please.' Give it to him. 'Clever boy!'

Again the best thing for you to do is eat the alternative so that it is no longer there to provoke an incident, but you should not have trouble. By now this has become a kind of game. These are small incidents in which you have arranged things so that he can win, without any unpleasantness. All he had to do was show you which he preferred and you gave it to him. And told him he was clever or good into the bargain. It is not terribly difficult to organise it so that he feels he does have some weight and will be listened to, at any rate in these matters. But make sure you stay in control; get in first before he has a chance to bring out any defiant tricks.

By now your child is becoming accustomed to the 'question-answer-receive something' pattern. Many children use one or two

short phrases of their own accord which can be applied to all sorts
of different situations with only a very slight variation. If your
child is limited in his use of language, you could introduce a phrase
like that to him, aiming to enlarge the language at his disposal, in
the same way as you introduced 'milk or orange'. Now it is 'this
one, or that one?'.

'Do you want this one, or that one?' You hold this one near
him, and that one away from him, to demonstrate the difference
in meaning. When he shows you which one he wants you say,
'This one, please', or 'That one, please', according to which it
was. As you speak you give it to him, emphasising *this*, and *that*.
Wait until he uses the phrases more or less correctly himself before
going on to introduce other words into the phrase. The list is
endless.

In this way we can teach the comparison of opposites — 'The
big one or the little one?', 'The thick one or the thin one?', 'The
long one or the short one?', 'The round one or the straight one?'.
To avoid confusion keep to one kind of object, so that he chooses
between a big banana and a little banana, for instance, not between
a banana and an orange. Then the only difference will be in the
size, which will need to be noticeable enough to make a proper
contrast so that he remembers which is which and keeps the
meaning of the significant words for later use.

Learning to follow instructions

You want to improve your child's understanding so that what he
pictures or says in his mind leads him to take the **right course of
action.** 'Now put your things away' does not bring a picture to
mind in the same way as 'Now put your things in the box', which
is easier to understand. He is familiar with the box, but he may
need practice in 'put them in' and similar phrases, not realising
that they tell us where things belong or where to find them.

'Where are you sitting?' 'On the chair.'
'Where are you standing?' 'Behind the chair.'
'Where are you standing now?' 'In front of the chair.'
'Put the car in the basket.'
'Take it out of the basket.'
'Put the car under the table.'

'Now stand in between the chair and the table.' And 'next to', and
'in front of', and all the other words to do with position which you
have used plus any more you can think of. In this way teach him

inside, outside, up, down, along, into, on top of, above, below, upstairs, downstairs, through, and so on.

Learning to reason

The everyday stuff of conversation is what we use for sorting and filing information in our memory so that we can find it again when we want it. It helps us **make sense** of our environment. The details and differences, for instance between 'yours', 'mine' and 'hers', convey the meaning of the conversation and how the people concerned stand in relation to each other. Using the familiar question and answer technique, practise conversations with your child, beginning with familiar phrases:

'Where are you sitting?' 'I am sitting on the floor.'
'What have I got in my basket?' 'It is a rabbit.'
'What am I taking out of my basket?' 'The rabbit.'
'Ask the rabbit what he wants to eat.' 'What do you want to eat, rabbit? He wants some lettuce.'
'Does he want a cake?' 'No, he doesn't want a cake.'
'Has he got a name? Ask him.' 'What's your name, rabbit? He says his name is Bunny.'
'Does this coat go on the rabbit?' 'No, it's too small.'
'Whose coat is it?' 'It's the doll's.'
'Is it yours?' 'No, it's not mine, it's hers.'

If your child does not answer some of these questions, you supply the answer for him. If he finds he has to use proper names instead of 'yours', 'hers', etc, he needs practice at games like this one. You can make up questions and invent a silly voice or puppet to take the pain out of repetition. (Use a sock and sew two buttons on the toe for eyes. Put your thumb in the heel and fingers in the toe to make it talk.)

Learning the words for self-control

You can make a game, too, out of teaching your child the words he will need in order to **control himself** and his actions. Drive small cars along plastic belts, saying 'Fast', 'Slow', 'Careful', 'Stop'. Lay the belts so that they make a crossroads and practise slowing down, stopping, and looking for traffic. Drive a car along a belt on the bedclothes saying, 'Up. Down. Round the corner.' Draw roads on a large piece of cardboard, and drive cars along them without going off the edge of the road, stopping at the crossings. Practise driving from one edge of the board to the other

without changing hands. Put in traffic lights and say, 'Get ready
to stop. Stop.' 'Get ready to go. Go.' Resist the temptation to play
crashes; just now we are very strong on respect for the law, and
likely to stay that way, too!

Draw road lines on sheets of paper, ie double lines the width of
his toy cars, and mark traffic lights at suitable points with a felt
pen. Draw arrows along some roads to show they are one-way. Let
the child drive his cars along the roads, practising obeying the
arrows and stopping at the lights. By these means he is learning
to control his *actions* according to instructions.

He can learn to control *himself*, too, as well as his actions. Draw
less wide, slightly wavy double lines (roads) on paper and let him
practise with a felt pen going from left to right down the middle
of the road, stopping at the traffic light at the right hand side of
the page. Keep up the controlling words of 'Go. Get ready to stop.
Stop.' As he has more practice in controlling his hands, make the
'roads' gradually narrower, so that he has to pay more attention to
what he is doing. Keep on with the 'Go' and 'Stop'.

By now I think we are agreed that we want 'No' and 'Stop' to
become part of his thinking! He can practise saying them when he
drives his cars, stopping them. He can tell his toys to stop doing
something, saying 'No. Stop. Naughty.' Out walking, you can both
say, 'Get ready. Stop.' when you reach the edge of the road before
crossing over. 'Can we go now?' 'No. Wait.' In the park, play
running and stopping. 'Go!' 'Stop!' Sometimes you give the order,
sometimes he does. In the kitchen, play the drums with old
saucepans and wooden spoons. 'Go!' ... 'Stop!' If you see
something you do not like when the television is on say, 'No!' or
'Stop!'; say it firmly, as if you mean it, and teach him to say it too.
If there are scenes of fighting say, 'No! Stop! We don't like that',
and switch off. And if he begins to wind himself up into a tantrum,
get in quickly with 'No! Stop!' and tell him to say it as well. The
more practice in stopping ordinary events he has, the better he will
remember the routine when he finds himself becoming upset. It
is still important to keep to using the same words each time in this
particular connection.

Increasing language skills

If he has truly spent a lot of his time in friction and uproar, it is
unlikely that he will have occupied many happy hours on a doting
knee looking at picture books or having stories read to him. When
we tell stories, look at books, sing or recite nursery rhymes with

children, we may think we are doing nothing more than telling a story. But the story or poem itself carries words and ideas through which we pass to the child traditional attitudes to other people, expectations of the family about behaviour, values, morality, all using a host of words for describing, measuring, comparing, counting and so on. Our child, wriggling unwillingly on the knee, may have failed to absorb some of these fundamental words which he needs to be able to use if he is to **reason problems out for himself.** By making a beginning, teaching him to choose between one simple drink and another and so on, we can lead him to develop this important vocabulary. Try the stories and rhymes again, encouraging valuable close contact with him at a time of day when there are not too many demands being made. He may find he enjoys them now. As his understanding grows, so will his independence, and we should see fewer signs of acute frustration.

Then there are endless jobs to do around the house, such as tidying up or laying the table, which need not be chores but a kind of game to play together in which you give practice either in the use of words you want him to adopt for himself, or just in doing what you say without ructions. However, make sure the vital phrases for self control are well practised — collecting opposites is a start: day/night; hot/cold; nice/nasty; good/bad; yes/no; do/don't; go/stop.

You may find it helpful to keep a record or diary of what you do each day so that you have a clear picture of the language you are building up, eg

3rd June
Cars: Go. Get ready to stop. Stop.
Pavement: Go. Get ready to stop. Stop. Get ready to go. Go.
Home: Hot/cold. Wet/dry. In/out. Go/stop. (Referring to cooker, taps, washing machine.)
  In the box. In the bag. In the bin. In the washing machine.

COOPERATION THROUGH PLAY

We can see from what we have covered so far that by playing with him like this we do more than practice the language which is related to these activities. We are also practising doing agreeable things in a **cooperative way**, using language both to describe what we are doing and also to help him control his actions. He is achieving more than he used to because what we are doing is making sure he pays close attention and does what we tell him to do. We establish it in small things and take care to keep the same system going in bigger things. And we are playing, not drumming it into him!

We can develop the cooperative aspect of play in ways which are enjoyable to him and which also let him know that we can find pleasure in his company. Sit with him at the table and help him do a puzzle (don't expect him to get on with it while you do something else). Show him how to find a corner and look for the piece that goes next to it by colour as well as shape. Take his hand and guide him to place it the right way round to fit. Say, 'Turn it round a little and see if it goes in that way.' Show him by moving his hand. 'Turn it round. Clever boy.' 'Find a green piece to go next to this one. The same as this one. Now look at the picture on the lid. What do we want to put in here?' and so on. All the time you are building on his language skills and teaching him close cooperation by example.

Here are some other simple activities which encourage co-operation as well as understanding:

- Building with bricks (following instructions, counting, noticing the differences). 'Put the red one on top of the blue one. Good. Now put the yellow one on the red one.' 'Make a tower the same as mine.' 'Make a tower of three bricks.'

- Find one 'like this', showing colour, shape or size (only one of the three to start with).

- Find the stranger, eg find the red one among several blue ones.

- Find the big one among the small ones.

- Find the bead among the bricks, the button among the beads, the triangle among the squares. Use the proper names to describe them, but also say 'Like this' if he is confused.

- Threading large beads, first just threading them, then copying another short thread of two or three beads by shape or colour. Encourage him to talk about the beads he is looking for as he does the threading.

- Sorting things into groups; forks, spoons, saucers, cups, pots, lids, things for the cupboard, the fridge, the drawer.

- Sorting clothes for the washing machine, 'White things here. Coloured things there.'

- Pairing cups with saucers, plastic bottles with tops, plastic boxes with lids.

- Laying the table. 'A knife for you, and a knife for me . . .'

- Sorting some of the ironing to be put away; things to go upstairs, things to stay downstairs.

IMPROVING SELF CONCEPT

In encouraging the child to develop a **positive self concept** we have two aims in view:

- To give him a more accurate idea of his size in relation to other people and how much space he needs between himself and objects; to give him greater awareness of his shape, strength and appearance.

- To help him to see himself as someone who can do things right, someone who is liked, who is strong, who is all the things we like him to be, even if we can only keep it up some of the time just now and still have to be ready to pounce.

Deliberately raising his self concept is surprisingly powerful provided you do it honestly. It is no good pretending that he has been helpful all morning if really he has been a little toad, because he is not silly. He knows perfectly well that you are trying to butter him up and will reward you by doubling the ransom or blackmail demand in return. But his recognition of himself as a separate being who has a say, though not the only one, in what happens is part of his being able to see himself as a respected contributor to the family.

Physical awareness
You can do exercises together to increase your child's **awareness of his body** and its relationship to the space around him:

'Stand up tall.'
'Reach up as high as you can.'
'Reach out sideways as wide as you can.'
'Reach out in front as far as you can.'

'Make yourself fat.' (Circular movement of the arms)
'Make yourself thin.' (Squeeze arms to sides)
'Curl up as small as you can.' (Into a ball)
'Touch your . . .' nose, chin, ears, knees, toes, elbows, and so on.
'Touch your left ear with your right hand.'
'Touch your right knee with your left hand.'

Such exercises will help him to learn coordination and control of his movements. If he is confused about left and right, try one of these:

● Sew R on his right glove and L on his left, and tell him what the letters stand for. Then ask him to show you which is which each time you give him something to do out of doors, eg turn to the right, turn to the left.

● Put his gloves down next to each other and show how the thumbs touch on the inside. Then look at his hands and find that they do the same. And his shoes or slippers. They look different from each other as well and he can see which side is the outside, just like his feet.

To increase his dexterity help him to practise, both with toy cars and when drawing, holding whatever he is using in one hand while he moves it right across in front of his body instead of changing hands. Don't fuss just now about which hand he prefers. Let him stand in front of a garden wall and draw lines in chalk right across, without moving his feet, from beyond his right side to beyond his left using the right hand, and back the other way using his left hand. Or, if large movements are difficult for him to manage, let him drive a car past the mid-line of his body, first with one hand and then the other.

Something we do *physically* with a child makes a more lasting impression than anything we simply talk about, and a good way of combining increased physical awareness with the habit of obeying instructions is to play 'do this, do that', where you both say and show what he has to do. (If you say 'do this' then he is supposed to copy you, but if he copies you when you say 'do that' then he is out and it is his turn to give you things to do — when your turn comes you will have to do as you are told, too!) The commands can be actions that you want him to get used to doing and which he can see how to do properly by your example as part of the game. 'Do this, sit on the chair.' 'Do that, stand up straight.' 'Do this, take off your coat.'

Similar games to play outside are statues or grandmother's footsteps. There is a variety of actions you can give the child — walking, running, hopping, walking on tiptoe, up the hill, down the hill, forwards, backwards, into the trees, out of the trees, round the bushes, and so on — but he always has to be ready to stop immediately, either by command or by following your example.

Your child needs to learn, too, about his strength and size in relation to the objects he uses. When you are in the park, talk about climbing up the ladder and going down the slide, see if he can squeeze between the rails of the climbing frame, whether he can fit into the spaces, how high he can reach, and every aspect of his size in relation to the apparatus he uses. If, because of the way he behaved in the past, he has not had much practice in climbing apparatus, see that he adjusts to heights by degrees. He may be unduly reckless, not realising how far he is from the ground, or fearful because he can see through the metal rails. He needs practice, and to know that he can stop himself falling by holding on tight if necessary.

There is an endless list of outdoor activities which you can use in the garden or in the park to help his coordination and control, again building on his increasing language skills. Tell him to climb, run, jump, hop, pull, push, throw, kick a ball — how? Fast, slow, with big steps, with little steps, forwards, backwards, sideways, on tiptoes — where? Over, out, behind, in front of, beside, at the back of, through, on top of, under.

- On the pavement, walk on the cracks and lines, or else between them.

- Draw a ladder on the path and walk in the spaces or on the rungs.

- Make stepping stones by laying leaves or flat stones on the grass, and then step from one to the other.

- Set up an obstacle course where he has to climb over and under something, slide on his tummy, walk on 'stepping stones' and so on.

If he didn't know it before, after a little practice he will realise that he has capability in all these activities and that you enjoy playing at them with him. His vocabulary will have been widened and been given more significance too. So although all of this looks rather far from direct interference in a tantrum, we can be fairly sure the use of language appropriate to the actions, and the growing awareness of himself as a separate person will work quietly like yeast. Eventually we will see the benefit because he will realise that he is capable of a different and more satisfying performance.

Personality

What we want to do is to let the child know, through all his contacts with the family but especially with his mother, that he is loved without question, just for himself, no matter what he does. What he does may not always be liked, but his actions are separate from himself. He needs to be shown, by the way he is treated, that no matter whether he is in or out of favour he can always be sure of being loved — stopping him when he does something wrong is part of your love for him. His interests are more important to you than whether he is pleased with you or not ('I always love you though I may not always like what you do.').

Once you can put a stop to disruptive behaviour, you can then be far gentler with him in everything you do than was possible while he was running riot. It is worth the hassle, just to experience being able to indulge him in little things, not spoiling him but letting him feel he is welcome company and liked, more often than letting him feel he is a pain. Smile when you greet him, let him see he can make you happy. It may stretch the imagination at times to think of him like this, but it paves the way for a kinder relationship and is worth the initial effort. It is self-perpetuating once you have begun — just as disruption can be.

There are many things you can do for him and with him so that he can begin to see that he is a **separate and valued personality** who can contribute to family life, rather than just a problem around whom the family revolves.

● Cook things he likes, as well as those things which are good for him.

● Cook things *together* — there is a simple recipe on the next page suitable for a child to help with.

● Let him help clean up afterwards, and be appreciative of his efforts.

● Let him choose where you go for a walk, what games you play.

● Make a kite *with* him, not for him. Have fun together flying it.

● Choose things for him to do which show him that he is capable, clever, strong, kind, lovable, so that he is encouraged to think of himself in this way.

● Give him lots of things to do that he likes doing, and praise him to others for how well he has done them. Take his photo in action.

Scotch Pancakes or Drop Scones

Ingredients
4 oz self raising flour
2 tablespoons sugar
1 egg, beaten
¼ pint milk

Method
Lightly grease a heavy frying pan.
Mix flour and sugar, making a well in the centre.
Stir in the egg, with enough milk to make a batter like thick cream. Do not beat the mixture.
Drop in spoonfuls onto the hot pan.
When bubbles come to the surface and burst, turn with an egg lifter and do the other side for a minute or two until light brown.
Place the cooked pancakes on a clean teatowel, folding it over the pancakes to keep the steam in.
Grease the pan again before starting on the next lot.
Eat while still warm, just as they are, or allow to cool and spread with butter and jam or cream, according to your current diet.
They should keep for a day in a tin.

● These are excellent for playing 'biscuit or pancake?' (see section on **Learning to choose** earlier in the chapter) and also give children a chance to make something for other people.

● *Just be with him*, quietly reading your book while he amuses himself, keeping each other company without the need to talk.

BUILDING TRUST AND CONFIDENCE

For a fair part of the time our child has behaved in a way that suggests he does not trust us to attend to him adequately nor to his needs. We have not been able to give much attention to this so far because we started out with an overwhelming behaviour problem which had to be brought under control first. However, by now we should have time for other activities which are more relaxed and which allow us to attend to the quality of our **physical and emotional contact** with the child, as part of our relationship and communication rather than as a means of control. In different circumstances this aspect would of course, have come first in any discussion about children.

Children who develop without serious problems in early childhood learn from the sensations they experience through their skin, when they move their bodies, and when they are held or moved by adults. They find out, through feeling, the difference between warmth and cold, softness and hardness, and whether the hands that hold them are kind or not. By experience they discover what their own strength is in relation to that of other people and, as they grow, how far they can risk themselves in strange situations, climbing trees, for instance. They learn about balance, running, jumping, and taking part in ordinary rough and tumble without getting too many bumps and bruises. They enjoy being thrown up in the air and being caught, held upside down, swung round, and trusting themselves to an adult to take care of them. Their excited laughter tells us that they enjoy a certain amount of danger, but only so much.

In some ways the world of the disruptive child is not the same as that of children without such problems, who appear to see the people around them as sympathetic, and do not spend a lot of time in conflict. Where there is a lot of behaviour disturbance it sometimes happens that a child misses the kind of relaxed physical experience referred to in the last paragraph. Once he starts school he looks too big to take part in such babyish activities as being thrown about by an adult, and in any case what adult could do it? Having missed this, though, he may seem clumsy and slow when taking part in ordinary physical education at school. This may lead to his being unwilling to take part in everything the others do, just when he needs both to join in and also to experience what they are enjoying.

If you suspect that this is the case you might embark on some floor exercises with your child, both to give him the exercise and also to build his confidence:

- Sit facing each other. Lean forward and hold hands, and then rock backwards and forwards. He will find that you hold him and don't let him fall back onto the floor, and that he is strong enough to do the same for you. He also finds that you trust him to hold you safe.

- Sit on the floor, legs apart, with him close to you, his back to you, and hold him cradled against you while you rock him from side to side. Let him rock you in the same way.

- Both of you lie on the floor and rest. Feel how heavy your legs and arms are. You pick up his legs, one at a time, and let them drop, and the same with his arms. He does the same for you. Sink into the floor.

- Perhaps you can find somewhere where you can roll and slide about on the floor together, pulling each other by the feet or arms, or play on an inflatable with him.

In all these ways he will learn that he is actually strong enough to move you about, and that he is a fair weight himself. These exercises may not lead to any great weight loss for either of you, but they will help him to become aware of sensations in his own body and the feeling of having the strength, as well as the ability to do as much for you as you can do for him. This is basic non-verbal communication, and at the same time a physical experience of mutual trust which will increase his confidence. It allows him to see himself as someone with the power, not to wreck everything, but to take care of another person, in this case you. The activity lends itself to making up songs and it brings an atmosphere of peace which he needs as much as you do.

These activities will not translate immediately into wonders in the gym at school, but they will contribute to his general well-being. He will see himself as being of greater worth because he has the strength to hold you and take care of you, that he is not just a person who has to receive from others all the time, but one who has something to give them. His self esteem lifts as he thinks of himself in a positive way.

CREATING A QUIETER CLIMATE

Quite apart from concentrating on the child there is much that parents can do to improve the general situation, whether by changes to their own attitude or the way they handle things, or by changes in the home environment.

Even the quickest of thinkers can, without too much trouble, slow down the speed of their speech. We can deliberately move more slowly and quietly. We can choose to ignore the fact that someone is ready to blow up, and behave towards them as if they were perfectly still and calm. We can reassure people by the way we look at them and our tone of voice, by going out of our way to look and sound sympathetic. Nurses do it to make frightened, sick people feel safer. It will do our child good too, by creating a more **restful, peaceful atmosphere.**

We can practise not reacting to situations that usually wind us up. Everyone is made to jump with irritation by something or other — sniffing, slurping tea, talking with food in the mouth, scraping shoes along the pavement, just the way he bangs the door. It's a useful exercise in self control to see if you can manage to ignore the offending habit for a short time — look upon it as survival training; learning to endure torture. Again, it will help to create a less confrontational atmosphere.

When we have to say something we know our child does not want to hear, we can help him to accept it by moving closer, putting a hand on his arm, patting his hand or stroking his cheek, or by letting him see that we do feel affection for him by our expression and voice. When he knows we respect his feelings he will not feel cornered by what it is we are saying. We can also reassure him by letting him see that even though he is in a pretty threatening mood we ourselves are not disturbed by it. We have to give him our attention, but it can be done so that it betrays no reaction to nervousness or irritability coming from him. If the situation escalates beyond a certain point then of course we have to take stronger action, but most of the time the fewer fireworks there are the better.

If your child is unable to understand or respond to language very well, it is probably best to introduce an unpopular event quietly, in small bites if at all possible. That way he is not faced with something all in one go which he simply cannot tolerate and which you can't explain to him. He can only benefit from having an ongoing peaceful atmosphere surrounding him, even if he does not enjoy some of the things which happen to him.

5
The Restless Child

The **restless child** seems disruptive not because he opposes on principle everything someone else suggests to him, but because he behaves like a whirlwind, unable to settle for long enough to concentrate, and unsettling everything in his vicinity. He does not finish anything he starts and spends most of his time disturbing everyone near him. He is attracted to whatever his eye lights on, but if he spots something else as he reaches for what he first saw he becomes drawn irresistibly to that instead. He may be supposed to be showing you something he has found, but no sooner has he begun doing so than his eyes are looking out of the window, following something there. Needless to say, he forgets what it was he was saying to you. When he starts doing something he does not attend to it once he has begun but is off again. He can't walk — he runs, climbs, rushes. If you are in the way he treads on your feet without noticing. He picks his toys up but does not always play with them and may drop them without apparently paying any attention to what he is doing. You start playing a game with him but you have to keep reminding him to watch the game, even to take his turn. When you do remind him, he attends for a short while. He does not make a fuss or resist unless you do something to restrain him from wriggling and fidgeting, then he may object.

You could not call him naughty, because he does not set out to annoy other people, nor does he aim to defy or hurt them. He is enthusiastic about what is in his mind at the moment, but it does not stay there long enough for him to achieve anything satisfactory to himself. Things get broken or spilt, but it is because of rushing and not looking rather than from temper or malice. Accidents just seem to happen as part of the day. He cannot control his responses to all the things he sees and hears around him. He is attracted by colour or brightness and often seems to misjudge the size, shape, or weight of the object he is interested in at the moment. If something is broken, like ornaments or china, it does not matter as much to him as it does to you because he does not think of the value in the same way.

Whether he receives medication or not, there is much parents can do to help an extremely restless, disruptive child themselves. Here we start by changing some aspects of the environment, to produce a quieter background for the child's activities. We then go on to using teaching methods which are similar to those suggested in the last chapter, but at times using a much more direct approach. It must be emphasised again that there can be no progress unless the child receives his fair share of love and enjoyment out of his contact with you, even when you are trying to stop him behaving in a certain way.

CUT DOWN ON THE DISTRACTIONS

For the sake of peace it is sensible to ban a child who cannot resist grabbing things from the room with your best furniture and ornaments, at least until he is better able to cope. In the rest of the house, even though he may be well over the age when most children try to touch everything, life will be easier for him and you if you can remove as many tempting objects as possible from within his reach — pictures, calendars, cards, photographs, vases, books, TV, radio, and anything else he can touch and which lends itself to being picked up and dropped, or bumped into and knocked over. If he is very young you could follow the example of a previous generation and put him in a play pen at times when you are unable to attend to him, for example when you are cooking. He can still be near you and he may be better off sitting on the floor with things to play with than jumping up and down in a baby bouncer, hanging from the lintel, and not being able to reach his things. Don't be horrified at the suggestion of a play pen. We can't all handle complete freedom all the time, and that includes him. We all need boundaries. As we grow up we learn to impose our own and that is what we want him to do. Resist the temptation to get into the play pen yourself and let everyone else get on with it!

Clear temptations out of his way, and not only will you not

have to protect your belongings from him all the time, but he will also be free from all the stimulating messages with which these things keep bombarding him. Because we have been used for so long to allowing children as much freedom as we can give them, this may look like punishment. But life can't be much fun for him or you if you are forever chasing him to retrieve your precious objects. Once you set about teaching him to *attend* only to those things which he chooses to notice, one at a time, and to *ignore* the invitations of the rest, keeping everything out of reach or out of sight won't have to last long. Comfort yourself with the thought that stripping the living area is the first step towards a more civilised way of life for all of you. And your privation can be used to encourage tidy habits in him, with toys put away properly, which will all help to give the home a more restful atmosphere.

The office
A child who is easily distracted can be helped by making a kind of 'office' for him — closing off the ends of the table where he sits, perhaps with hardboard or cardboard, to reduce further the amount he sees out of the corner of his eye. These sides act rather like blinkers, except that they are not close enough to make him feel shut in. The idea came from researchers who gave children

cubicles to work in as an aid to concentration. Such cubicles are now found in many libraries and they certainly do help people who would otherwise keep noticing movements when they are trying to attend to something.

While the cubicle or 'office' might not have been designed for children who behave in a disruptive manner, it can be used to advantage with them too. Your child might be more successful building with bricks, doing a puzzle, or looking at a book, if you were able to **reduce the distractions** in this way.

LEARNING TO CONCENTRATE

As well as cutting down on distractions and arguments about breakages, you want to help the child **pay attention** to activities designed to teach him specific things. At present he cannot do this because he can't shut out the many interruptions to thought. This means that he cannot at present concentrate on one item at a time.

You want him to feed himself without spilling — he must learn to think about getting the spoonful to his mouth, and nothing else, until that is done. It is no use fussing because he makes a mess; that causes him to look away from the spoon. Cover the floor with newspaper instead, cover the table with a plain plastic cloth that can be wiped, and tie a napkin around his neck. Now, one thing at a time. Just get the spoon to his mouth. Don't talk about anything else while he is doing that. Isn't he clever? Next, the food off the spoon and safely inside the mouth! It doesn't matter whether he is a baby or an older child, the process is the same. Some mothers are so upset by the inevitable mess at this stage that they insist on feeding the child themselves when he is about ten months old. Then, three months later, they are annoyed because he shows no interest in picking up the spoon for himself. Proof that at least some of what we do makes an impression.

Feeding himself is harder than it looks to us. The child has to be quiet. He has to sit still for a relatively long time. He has to look at the plate and not put his hand in the food. He has to pick up the spoon the right way round, load it and carry it to his mouth with precision, so that he can put the food in the right place. And so on. If, from where he sits, he can see out of the window, or kick his brother, hear the radio or see the television, his attention will be divided and he will not be able to concentrate on his plate and spoon. If the table and surroundings are full of books and magazines, pots and pans, cats, hamsters, toys, plants, tropical fish and general clutter, then he hasn't got a hope. All of those will act on his eyes, hands and ears like magnets.

He might do a lot better sitting beside you, alone, facing a bare wall, with only one plate in front of him, and that plate holding just a little food which is easy to scoop up in a spoon, and which he likes. You don't want him to look at you but at the plate. You don't want any unnecessary noise, because he has to concentrate on the task in hand. If you think he won't be able to manage the whole job alone at first, then help him get it right. Load the spoon for him by holding your hand over his and then guide his hand, the right way up, to his mouth.

Carry on helping him to feed himself only as long as he is able to pay attention, even if it is for not more than a minute. You want him to increase the length of time he pays attention because he finds it worth his while. As soon as his attention flags, you take over, telling him he is clever to have done so much, and then finish spooning in the rest yourself. Keep it good-natured. Take a photo of him while he puts the spoon in his mouth and pin it up as an encouragement, above where he has his meals. Show him you expect he will want to do it for himself at the beginning of every meal. Remember only to offer a small, manageable amount for him to tackle on his own and don't go off and leave him to it. Privately only expect him to manage one spoonful alone at the beginning of each meal, but be overjoyed at any sign of cooperation even if it is not too successful. As soon as he shows he can get on fairly well step aside, but be ready to take over as soon as his interest goes. You don't want a battleground over food, so only ask a little and be pleased with small signs of progress. As in other things, little and often achieves more than a great long uphill slog. Leave knives and forks out of the plan until other, more important things are sorted out. Only offer him food which is easy to pick up with a spoon and which he likes.

Your teaching strategy
Getting him to feed himself may seem to be very simple, but in fact you are taking on quite a lot. First, there is the direction of attention to one thing while ignoring everything else. Then, planning to improve performance in one area at a time by dividing what you want him to do into very small steps. Then you take the steps in order so that each step is within his ability and he can be successful from the very start. That way you plan to be pleased

with him, instead of feeling you have to step in and put him right every half minute. Overall you want him to cooperate, which is why you manipulate what he does so that you can praise him. This is harder to plan that it seems and so it is worth jotting down the steps with pencil and paper.

Aim: To feed himself

Needed
1. To sit away from distraction from things he can see or hear.
2. Sensitive surfaces covered so that spills don't matter.
3. Spoon, plate with a rim to push against, non-slip plastic mat to stand plate on, small helping of something he likes and which is easy to pick up.
4. The rest of the serving near, to be given by adult.

Steps
1. Adult guides the child's hand to pick up the first mouthful, and guides it to his mouth. 'Clever boy. You try it now.'
2. Adult gives him the spoon the correct way for him to pick up some food. Adult makes suitable noises to encourage him, and sees he gets the food in the spoon.
3. Adult is ready to take over at the first suspicion of wandering attention rather than spark a row.
4. Adult finishes feeding the child.

Lay on the 'Clever boy!' a bit to get things moving. If you can keep this training up every day you will win in the end, so don't despair! If he kicks up a fuss be quick to stop the fuss, but make no connection between bad behaviour and his eating his food. If he is not hungry, that is quite OK with you and you do not try to persuade him. You can start in the same way again later. Don't bribe him by offering ice cream when he has refused the first course, especially if that was something he asked for — if he is not hungry, that means not hungry for any food. Don't punish him either by bringing out the rejected meal at the next mealtime and telling him to eat it. Or yell at him, even if you feel like it.

The method you used for planning the feeding strategy and putting it into practice can also be used to teach him all sorts of things:

Aim: To wash his face for himself

Needed
Plug in, water in basin, face cloth squeezed out ready.

Steps
1. Adult washes his face for him, carefully.
2. He looks in mirror to see how he looks.
3. Adult dries his face for him.
4. He pulls plug out and rinses the basin.

The child takes over one step at a time from the adult, working backwards from (4) instead of forwards.

Aim: To get undressed by himself

Steps
1. Get him to take off his shoes.
2. Move on to socks and shoes.
3. Pants, socks and shoes.
4. Shirt, pants, socks and shoes.

And so on, adding one item at a time.

Aim: To see to himself in the toilet

Steps
1. To wash his hands.
2. To flush the loo.
3. To pull up his pants.
4. To wipe his bottom.

Again the child learns one step at a time, working from the last and simplest step and adding the next one to the sequence as soon as he has managed the previous one.

LEARNING THROUGH PLAY

Everything you want him to do needs your attention and planning, especially so that you do not become irritated by his failure to complete tasks. You do not want him to remain in a state of permanent excitement either, so you may have to tell him quite firmly what to do, and see that he does it. Say, 'Look at me. Look at my eyes. Now, listen!' Put your fingers gently under his chin to get him to look at you. Then give only one instruction at a time. 'Do this', and show him.

He may not play with his toys in an appropriate way, throwing little cars about rather than pretending to drive them along a road. Although you understand that a toy car represents a real one it may not mean the same to him. He may need you to sit next to him at the table and show him how we play with a little car and the noises we make, pretending that he is in it and saying where he is going. That way he enters a game of make believe which he can share with other children as well as adults. He does not want more than one toy, and he does not want to look at you but to fix his attention, even for a short time, on the car. It is useful to have several other items ready, but out of sight, in a basket by your side so that when he has tired of the first toy after a minute or two you can put that one away and bring out another.

By **holding his attention** in this way, producing one small thing after another, you are still helping him to subdue the temptation to flit to things outside his field of vision and at the same time teaching him, by degrees, to sit still. Once he has accepted the idea of sitting still and attending for a little while you can give practice at placing things in front of, behind, next to each other, and so on, as suggested in the last chapter. The only talking you want to encourage is for him to say what he is doing because that reinforces his memory of how it was done. Afterwards you can ask him what you and he did and how he did it. You want to encourage him to repeat words which will help him concentrate and improve his own control of his actions by becoming associated in his mind with the activity. Don't be tempted to keep him at it too long, but if he can say, 'Drive along the road and stop at the corner', with the toy car, he should be able to say it even if you are not there. The words direct his actions. One day he might tell himself not to do something because it is naughty.

If your child seems to have difficulty in following your instructions you should be careful to make your own statements very clear, simple and short. Speak clearly, holding your face close to his. Turn his face towards you by placing your fingers under his chin. Use the same phrases for the same things every time you tell him to do something (keep a diary if you need a memory aid). Keep to the same order each time you sit together at the table to do something. Take his hand and see that he does it right, giving praise when he does. Three minutes of success is worth fifteen of struggle. By preventing mistakes you save him from disappointment. If you can keep to a short routine once or twice a day you will prepare the ground for teaching him to wait his turn at table, say 'Please' and 'Thank you', and begin leading him to behave in a way which allows others to like him instead of trying to avoid him. Sitting at table alone with you and learning to concentrate is the most valuable thing he can do just now, but he needs a lot of practice.

LEARNING PATIENCE

So far this child has received a lot of attention, one way and another, for a long time. At first it was for all the wrong reasons and we had to put a stop to that by directing our energy into more productive channels. We have had to insist that he fulfils his part of the bargain, and it has taken time to set up better patterns of behaviour. Of course it is not right for one child to dominate our time and attention, especially if there are other children in the house, but it is only when things are running pretty smoothly that we can safely look at ways of reducing the time devoted by adults to the child, although we will still have to put a stop to any backsliding as soon as it threatens.

You could describe this child as having a low tolerance for frustration. He does not like 'No', nor even 'Just a minute'. He has had everyone jumping every time he shouts, for long enough to think that that was the right way to live his life. But by this time he has done quite a lot of changing, not all of it a battle either. He has even come in for a fair amount of praise while we have been laying the foundations.

We could lift the ban on sweets or some other small bribe while we are concentrating on his **patience.** We want a weapon that is not connected with good or bad behaviour, just something he likes which we can use for our own purposes. The plan is to give him one or two sweets after lunch just because you happen to have them, and to extend the time between the end of lunch and giving him the sweets very gradually so that he does not become impatient. After a week or so you should be able to delay four or five minutes, saying to him, 'Just a minute and I'll give you a sweet'. He has to be sure you won't forget and if he is worried you could set the kitchen timer to make sure. By degrees he should be able to accept being told, 'In five minutes'.

This leads to putting things ready for his morning drink and snack but inserting a short delay before giving them to him. The words you want him to get used to are, 'Wait a minute', 'I'm coming', 'I'm nearly ready', or 'We'll have it in five minutes' and 'We'll set the timer'. If you keep him waiting too long in the beginning you will be forced into having to decide whether to give the drink to him or not because he has kicked up such a fuss over having to wait. He will learn faster if he knows it is not a long wait and that he always gets his due unless he misbehaves.

When applied to other daily events this helps the child to learn telling the time. Show him where the hands on the clock will be when it is lunch time and tell him what time that is. Let him see when the hands are coming to the time and try to serve the meal regularly. Do the same for the evening meal but concentrate on the time of only one meal until he is sure of it. When he has got hold of, say, midday and six o'clock, then go on to saying, 'We'll go for a walk at three o'clock'. Draw the hands for him. He can tell you when it is time to go. Don't be tempted to go early because it looks like rain until he has got the time sorted out. When you want him to wait five minutes, show him five minutes on the clock, after which time do whatever you said you would do. It comes to mean something then. In this you are teaching not only about the passage of time but also, more importantly, that he does not need to make a fuss to get you to do what you say you will. Once he knows he really will get the sweet, or his lunch, at the time you have said there is less reason for him to behave as if you intended to deprive him.

When he goes to bed you could give him a picture book or toy and tell him you will be up in five minutes to say goodnight. This is the beginning of his learning to do without you all the time. When you are going to be busy in the kitchen, first settle him properly with his building bricks or puzzle, where you can see him, and don't leave it too long before having a look to see how he is doing. Weaning takes thought, preparation, materials and time. He has to learn by degrees to wait, knowing that you will not forget him, and in the meantime to occupy himself without getting into a state.

WHAT ABOUT DIET?

Everyone has a theory about the part played by diet in behaviour problems, especially with the extremely restless child, but don't make the mistake of trying first this and then that, following what is being said in magazines. You could be given advice which conflicts as much as horoscopes do. Something in food may indeed be playing a part but whether it plays a **significant part** in the case of your child may take a long time to establish and more time again to find ways of correcting it. If you think that food may be contributing to the problem go and see someone who knows what they are talking about, starting with your doctor, but don't be tempted to go from one expert to another, hoping to find one who will give you an acceptable answer. This is the way we all tend to act; when we are worried it is natural to look for someone who will give us the kind of answer which relieves the worries, but it may be that there is no easy answer and you will simply have to continue to work on his behaviour.

While you are looking at alternatives you should not let things slide as far as behaviour goes, in any case. Anti-social behaviour is not acceptable whatever the reason.

Whether or not there is more to be done than you have been trying so far, keep up the good work. What you wanted to achieve in the first place — improved behaviour — was entirely reasonable.

YOUR INFLUENCE MAKES THE DIFFERENCE

No matter what we do we can't avoid influencing the way our children or pupils behave. They may seem to us to take no notice of anything we say, but all the time they are picking up our attitudes and mannerisms, and when they want to annoy us their observations have taught them what to do.

By thinking more consciously about what we really want to communicate to them we can make changes in *our own* behaviour which will in turn bring about changes in *theirs*. Part of our responsibility as parents is to set an example which will teach our children worthwhile values.

The endearing thing about young children is that they live in the present, acting spontaneously and unable to weigh up the consequences of their actions because they are preoccupied with what they are doing. That is why we must accept our own responsibility as adults and take charge when we see them doing something wrong, stop them, and show them the right way.

6
Sources of Help

SEEKING HELP

Don't be afraid to ask for help or advice. Don't think you are being a nuisance; the kind of people who may be able to help are paid to help. That's what they are there for. They wouldn't have anything to do if no-one consulted them. Don't think you will never be able to explain; they will have heard everything there is to hear. In any case their job is not to judge people but to see whether they have an idea, or something in their cupboard, or a phone number, which might be useful to you. Ring for an appointment first to make sure they will be there when you want to see them. Try people like:

● the **head of your child's school,** who will know educational and clinical psychologists;

● **Social Services,** who could ask one of their experienced staff to come and see you;

● **your GP**, who is interested in you as well as your child;

● the **community nurse** at your health centre, who could visit you.

Someone you meet through these contacts is likely to be able to help with training programmes and give you encouragement. Make your GP or health centre your first approach, and if you are worried insist on an assessment of your child by specialists. Point out that you need *practical* suggestions about what to do and ask for information about why your child's behaviour is so difficult to manage. If there is any question of a medical reason, ask to be referred to a **paediatrician** and request information about the diagnosis and what you can do yourself apart from the medication. You need to know whether the child is unwell or not. If he is not ill, ask to see someone from the child guidance clinic, preferably in your own home, for practical suggestions about management.

If it is not a medical matter, and you are given conflicting advice by different specialists, don't jump from one to the other. Settle for one and tell them what you are doing.

Go to your **area DSS** office yourself and find out what is available in the way of help, even if you do not need it just now. There might be a chance of a home help or short-term care, depending on your circumstances. Find out from them whether you qualify for an attendance allowance or mobility allowance if your child does have a medical condition. If you have to make a lot of hospital visits, ask the hospital social worker whether there is any help with transport.

There are plenty of other sources, too, and some useful addresses are given at the end of the chapter. Your **library** has probably got a list of groups who may be able to help, or just offer friendship. As well as directories of addresses, your library will probably have reference books and pamphlets which may be useful. There are all sorts of voluntary bodies, including self-help groups. In fact, if you don't find something that looks a possibility, what about putting an advertisement in the local paper and starting your own group?

Then there is the **Citizens' Advice Bureau**. You may not find an expert on duty in the office when you drop in, but they will be able to put you in touch with someone.

So, one way and another, you should find you are not the only one — a great relief, even if all you do, once you have found a kindred spirit, is babysit for each other and drink coffee together.

TAKING ADVICE

Don't be swamped
When you have found someone who can give advice, just remember to use your survival antennae. Don't leave it so long before going that by the time you meet them you are exhausted and dis-

heartened. If you leave it until you are down, you may just take what they say without thinking first whether it is **right for your own circumstances**.

Experts are expert at all sorts of different problems. You are a specialist in your own problem and will have to tell them in detail what is wrong. Think carefully about their advice before putting it into practice, and if you think that it is all wrong in your circumstances tell them so. Explain why you think so, not to play a game with them to show how impossible your situation is, but to make the position clearer.

Help them to help you
Let them know what you have tried and how you have got on, showing them any notes or charts, so that they can see you have already tackled it sensibly and laid some good foundations. Use your common sense in seeing that they have the **right information** so that you can use *their* brains.

Tell them what you want from them
Go with the **right attitude,** not just to show them you are smarter than they are (even if you are), nor to prove your problem is the worst they have ever met. Use your initiative; make some notes about what is troubling you (and remember to take them with you). You want to find out as much as possible about your child's behavioural problems and the reasons for them but, more importantly, what you and others can do to *help* him.

USEFUL ADDRESSES

The addresses given here are for head offices. There will be branches of most societies throughout the UK and Ireland, and one call will get you the number of your nearest branch.

Association of Parents of Vaccine-Damaged Children, 2 Church Street, Shipston on Stour, Warwicks CV36 4 AP (tel: 0608-61595).

British Diabetics Association, 10 Queen Anne Street, London W1M OBD (tel: 01-323 1531).

British Dyslexia Association, 98 London Road, Reading, Berks RG1 5AU (tel: 0734-668271/2).

British Epilepsy Association, 40 Hanover Square, Leeds LS3 1BE (tel: 0532-439393).

British Institute of Mental Handicap, Wolverhampton Road, Kidderminster, Worcs DY10 3PP (tel: 0562-850251). Information and resource centre; can answer questions on all aspects of mental handicap.

Campaign for Mentally Handicapped People, 16 Fitzroy Square, London W1P 5HQ (tel: 01-387 9571). Deals with issues to do with living in the community.

College of Speech Therapists, Harold Poster House, 6 Lechmere Road, London NW2 5BU (tel: 01-459 8521/3). Will send pamphlets and advise where to go for local help.

Contact a Family, 16 Strutton Ground, London SW1P 2HP (tel: 01-222 2695/3969). Support groups for families whose children have special needs.

Down's Syndrome Association, 12–13 Clapham Common Southside, London SW4 7AA (tel: 01-720 0008).

Friends of the Young Deaf Trust, East Court Mansion, Council Offices, College Lane, East Grinstead, W Sussex RH19 3LT (tel: 0342-23444).

Gingerbread (Association for One Parent Families), 35 Wellington Street, London WC2 7BN (tel: 01-240 0953).

Hyperactive Children's Support Group, 71 Whyke Lane, Chichester, W Sussex PO19 2LD (tel: 0903-725182).

MENCAP (Royal Society for Mentally Handicapped Children and Adults), 123 Golden Lane, London EC1Y 0RT (tel: 01-253 9433). Deals with all aspects of mental handicap.

National Association for Maternal and Child Welfare, 1 South Audley Street, London W1Y 6JS (tel: 01-491 2772). Publishes leaflets and pamphlets on child rearing and parent-craft.

National Childminding Association, 8 Masons Hill, Bromley, Kent BR2 9EY (tel: 01-464 6164).

National Children's Bureau, 8 Wakely Street, London EC1V 7QE (tel: 01-278 9441).

National Deaf Children's Society, 45 Hereford Road, London W2 5AH (tel: 01-229 9272/4).

Play Matters (National Toy Libraries Association), 68 Churchway, London NW1 1LT (tel: 01-387 9592). Offers a support service to parents by making available and lending appropriate toys.

Pre-School Playgroups Association, 61-3 King's Cross Road, London WC1X 9LL (tel: 01-833 0991).

Royal National Institute for the Blind, 224-228 Great Portland Street, London W1N 6AA (tel: 01-388 1266).

Royal National Institute for the Deaf, 105 Gower Street, London WC1E 6AH (tel: 01-387 8033).

Scottish Down's Children's Association, 478 Anniesland Road, Glasgow G13 1YH (tel: 041-959 4305).

Scottish Society for the Mentally Handicapped, 13 Elmbank Street, Glasgow G2 4QA (tel: 041-226 4541).

Spastics Society, 12 Park Crescent, London W1N 4EQ (tel: 01-636 5020).

Further Reading

Coping Successfully With Your Hyperactive Child, Dr Paul Carson (Sheldon Press, 1987).

Coping With Young Children, Douglas and Richmond (Penguin, 1988).

Developmental Movement for Children: Mainstream, Special Needs & Pre-school, Veronica Sherborne (Cambridge University Press, 1990).

Down's Syndrome: A Guide for Parents, C. Cunningham (Human Horizons, 1988).

A Good Enough Parent: The Guide to Bringing up Your Child, B. Bettleheim (Pan, 1988). The author is a long-established authority, especially in the field of autism, but is also highly respected for his understanding of child development.

Helping Your Handicapped Child, Janet Carr (Penguin, 1980). Detailed text on behaviour modification, covering all aspects of child management.

How to Help Your Child at School, John West-Burnham (Northcote House, 1987).

How to Prepare Your Child for School, Jeanne L. Jackson (Northcote House, 1989).

Hyperactive Children: A Parent's Guide, Flack (Bishopsgate, 1987). Relates behaviour problems to diet, particularly artificial colourants, and sugar. Easy to read, but research has not yet established that all troubles can be attributed to diet.

If You Don't Behave, Bidder and Hewitt (Griffiths Test Agency, 1987). Written for parents, covering behaviour modification and early intervention.

Let Me Play, D. M. Jeffree et al (Human Horizons, 1985).

Let Me Read, D. M. Jeffree and H. Skeffington (Human Horizons, 1980).

Let Me Speak, D. M. Jeffree and R. McKonky (Human Horizons, 1976).

Let's Join In, D. M. Jeffree and S. Cheseldie (Human Horizons, 1984).

Let's Make Toys, D. M. Jeffree and R. McKonky (Human Horizons, 1981).

These books on parent guidance, arising out of work at the Hester Adrian Research Centre in Manchester, are all sound, and mostly readable without a knowledge of psychology.

Parent's Survival Guide, Laurie Graham (Chatto & Windus, 1986). Highly entertaining, illustrated with pen drawings. All sound common sense.

Problem Behaviour in People with Severe Learning Disabilities, Zarkowska and Clements. Standard behaviour modification text, by and for professionals.

Resources for Teaching Young Children With Special Needs, Penny Low Diener (Harcourt Brace Jovanovich, 1983). Gives detailed programmes for almost every aspect of a child's education. Comprehensive reference lists. Not specific about behaviour problems but illustrates how to assess and plan. Published in the USA, can be ordered from a library.

Working With Parents, C. Cunningham and Hilton Davis (Open University Press, 1985).

Your Child Needs You: A Positive Approach to Down's Syndrome, Joyce Mepsted (Northcote House, 1988).

Index